CW00551599

The *Roman Noir* in Post-War French Culture

OXFORD STUDIES IN MODERN EUROPEAN CULTURE

GENERAL EDITORS

Elizabeth Fallaize, Robin Fiddian, and Katrin Kohl

Oxford Studies in Modern European Culture is a new series conceived as a response to the changing modes of study of European literature and culture in many universities. Designed to combine focus with breadth, each title in the series will present a range of texts or films in dialogue with their historical and cultural contexts—not simply as a reflection of history but engaged in a mediation with history, conceived in broad terms as cultural, social, and political history. Flexible, interdisciplinary approaches are encouraged together with the use of texts outside the traditional canon alongside more familiar works. In order to make the volumes accessible not only to students of modern languages but also to those studying the history or politics of modern Europe, all quotations are offered in both the original language and English.

The *Roman Noir*

in Post-War French Culture

Dark Fictions

Claire Gorrara

OXFORD
UNIVERSITY PRESS

OXFORD
UNIVERSITY PRESS

Great Clarendon Street, Oxford OX2 6DP

Oxford University Press is a department of the University of Oxford.
It furthers the University's objective of excellence in research, scholarship,
and education by publishing worldwide in

Oxford New York

Auckland Bangkok Buenos Aires Cape Town Chennai
Dar es Salaam Delhi Hong Kong Istanbul Karachi Kolkata
Kuala Lumpur Madrid Melbourne Mexico City Mumbai Nairobi
São Paulo Shanghai Taipei Tokyo Toronto

Oxford is a registered trade mark of Oxford University Press
in the UK and certain other countries

Published in the United States
by Oxford University Press Inc., New York

British Library Cataloguing in Publication Data
Data available

Library of Congress Cataloging in Publication Data
Data available
ISBN 0-19-924609-2

10 9 8 7 6 5 4 3 2 1

Typeset by Graphicraft Limited, Hong Kong
Printed in Great Britain
on acid-free paper by
Biddles Ltd, Guildford and King's Lynn

Preface and Acknowledgements

This book would not have been possible without a Leverhulme Research Fellowship for 2001–2. This allowed me to make research trips to Oxford and Paris and gave me the time to complete the manuscript. I gratefully acknowledge the support of the Leverhulme Trust. I would also like to thank the School of European Studies, Cardiff University, for help in the form of sabbatical leave, with special thanks to colleagues in the French Section who covered my absence.

In terms of library and research facilities, I would like to thank staff at the Bibliothèque des Littératures Policières (BiLiPo) and the Bibliothèque Nationale in Paris, the British Library in London, and the Taylorian in Oxford. The staff at BiLiPo enabled me to make the most of my trips there, and I would like particularly to thank the library curator Catherine Chauchard for her suggestions in relation to this book, as well as her kind help with comparative projects around crime fiction.

Earlier versions of two chapters of the book have already appeared in print. A discussion of the Occupation in *Léo Malet's 120, rue de la Gare* from Ch. 1 was published in a modified form in *French Cultural Studies*, 12/3 (October 2001), 271–83. Some aspects of my analysis of Didier Daeninckx's *Meurtres pour mémoire* have appeared as '*Meurtres pour mémoire*: Remembering the Occupation in the Detective Fiction of Didier Daeninckx', *Journal of the Institute of Romance Studies*, 6 (1998), 353–9, reproduced in *Remembering and Presenting the Experience of War in Twentieth-Century France*, ed. Debra Kelly (Lampeter: Edwin Mellen Press, 2000), 131–40, and, in a comparative context, as 'Tracking Down the Past: The Detective as Historian in Texts by Patrick Modiano and Didier Daeninckx', in *Crime Scenes: Detective Narratives in European Culture Since 1945*, ed. Anne Mullen and Emer O'Beirne (Amsterdam: Rodopi, 2000), 281–90. Permission to reprint is gratefully acknowledged.

I would like to thank those colleagues and friends who have helped in the writing of this book, especially Colin Davis who agreed to read through a draft at fairly short notice. His support has been invaluable throughout the writing process. I would also like to thank David Platten who read a draft of the Introduction and gave insightful advice and suggestions. Thanks must also go to colleagues who participated in the conference 'Cultural Identities: Noir Fiction and Film in France and Italy', co-organized by

Giuliana Pieri and myself in April 2002. The lively debate in sessions helped to clarify much of my thinking. I am grateful to students on my 'French Detective Fiction and Film' course at Cardiff University, 2000–1; they were in many ways the guinea pigs for the ideas developed in this book and made the project lots of fun. It is also a great pleasure to thank friends and colleagues who have contributed with encouragement and help at different stages in the project: Margaret Atack, Delphine Cingal, Véronique Desnain, Hanna Diamond, Elizabeth Fallaize, Rachael Langford, Nick Parsons, Giuliana Pieri, and Joanna Stephens. I would also like to thank Patrick Raynal, current editor of the Série noire, for kindly agreeing to be interviewed. Throughout, unless otherwise indicated, all translations are my own.

Lastly, this book is dedicated to Joe Boyle who has read along with me, lived through the peaks and troughs of writing, and managed to remain a calming and supportive presence throughout. With love.

C.G.

London
April 2002

Contents

Introduction

Approaches to the *roman noir*

The *roman noir* occupies an ambivalent position in relation to post-war French culture. For many, it is associated with *paralittérature*, that is, popular forms of writing, such as science fiction or the romance, marginalized by the literary establishment. By conforming to the well-worn formulas of detective fiction, the *roman noir* seems to offer little more than consumer-driven pulp fiction aimed at less discerning readers. Cheap paperback collections, such as Gallimard's Série noire, have come to epitomize the *roman noir*'s reputation as salacious crime stories to thrill the senses and defy conventional morality.[1] However, for other critics, the impact of the *roman noir* goes way beyond the annals of popular culture. Developed in early twentieth-century America, it has been read as a formative cultural narrative for our times. Social historians and cultural critics have interpreted the story of the intrepid detective and his fight against crime as a modern-day epic.[2] The city itself becomes one of the main protagonists in tales of violence and transgression that probe readers' anxieties about the world in which they live. In France, this 'double' vision of the *roman noir*, as both pulp fiction and contemporary urban narrative, has been heightened by the cross-cultural origins of the form, as well as its infiltration of other media, particularly film. For if the beginnings of the *roman noir* can be traced to the hard-boiled novels of interwar American writers such as Dashiell Hammett, the concept of *noir* as a distinct corpus of books and films was invented by the French. With the arrival of American music, literature, and film after the Liberation of France in 1944, French readers immersed themselves in a wave of American culture.[3] Newly imported books and films were made all the

[1] See Thomas Narcejac, *La Fin d'un bluff: essai sur le roman policier noir américain* (Paris: Le Portulan, 1949), for a vehement critique of the first wave of American hard-boiled detective fiction to hit post-war France.

[2] See Francis Lacassin in *Mythologie du roman policier*, 2 vols. (Paris: UGE, 1974), ch. 8, 'Dashiell Hammett où la littérature à haute tension', 5–40. Lacassin discusses Hammett's fiction as a sort of biblical epic with immorality and corruption ruthlessly expunged and punished.

[3] See Robert E. Conrath, 'Pulp fixation: le roman noir américain et son lecteur français d'après-guerre', *La Révue génerale*, 12 (1995), 37–45, for a discussion of the American *roman noir* and its reception in immediate post-war France.

more exotic by four years of penury during which American products of all kinds had been banned by the German invader. This French reception of the *roman noir* was a foundational moment in the history of *noir* fiction and film, making the connections between narrative form and a dark socio-political vision that have become the hallmarks of *noir* ever since.

The aim of this book is to analyse a selection of French-authored *noir* narratives from the post-war period and to explore how they intersect with wider social and historical forces. The main emphasis will be on the *roman noir* but discussion of film adaptations will inform close textual readings and *film noir* will be the subject of one chapter. Authors have been chosen for the innovation of their work and the exciting ways in which they resist tired conventions and offer new ways of representing social realities. It is certainly not the contention of this book that all French *noir* fiction and film can be read in this manner. Much has been published that can be considered little more than a pale imitation of an American model. Yet, to relegate all such writing to the literary wasteland is to ignore the impact of a distinctive and widely disseminated corpus of texts on post-war French cultural identity. This introduction will set out some of the main approaches to the *roman noir*. It will examine the structures and narrative patterns associated with the *roman noir* before focusing on the cultural contexts in which such a form has evolved. The place of the *roman noir* in a wider history of French detective and crime fiction will conclude this Introduction, thus providing an overview of the main developments to be discussed in subsequent chapters.

Form and fiction

Some of the earliest critics of popular culture recognized that the detective story was distinguished from other popular forms, such as the adventure story, by a specific structure. Instead of a linear tale of action and terror culminating in the hero's victory, the detective story is built upon an inversion.[4] For the detective story begins with the discovery of a crime only to move back in time to reconstruct the circumstances that have led up to the discovery. The most influential study of forms of detective fiction appeared in 1966 with Tzvetan Todorov's 'Typology of Detective Fiction'.[5] Todorov's structuralist analysis provides a fully functioning

---

[4] See Roger Callois, 'Puissances du roman', in *Approches de l'imaginaire* (Paris: Gallimard, 1974), 177–205. This article was first published in 1941.

[5] Tzvetan Todorov, 'A Typology of Detective Fiction', in *The Poetics of Prose*, trans. Richard Howard (Oxford: Blackwell, 1977), 42–52.

description of detective fiction as a genre apart. He sets out to elucidate not only the basic premise of detective fiction as a narrative type but also to classify detective fiction along the lines of form and theme.

Todorov defines detective fiction as structured around two temporal sequences: the story of the crime and the story of the investigation: 'the first—the story of the crime—tells "what really happened," whereas the second—the story of the investigation—explains "how the reader (or the narrator) has come to know about it" '.[6] In other words, what previous critics had perceived to be an inverted story of discovery is in fact the coexistence of two narrative sequences that simultaneously pull the reader back in time to reconstruct a missing story of crime and forward in time to follow the processes of the investigation. This duality at the heart of the detective story acts as the fulcrum around which Todorov defines three different kinds of detective fiction: the whodunit, the thriller, and the suspense novel. For in each of these narratives, the relationship between the story of the crime and the story of the investigation is different, giving rise to variations in character, theme, style, and point of view.

The whodunit or classic mystery novel is predicated on the separation of the two stories with a crime committed prior to the opening of the narrative. In the whodunit, the detective works to assemble the clues, like a jigsaw puzzle, and to move towards a final summation when all falls into place. Todorov associates this type of detective fiction with a Golden Age of the genre published during the inter-war years and the work of British and American writers, such as Agatha Christie and Ellery Queen, and their 'country house' murder mysteries. Centred on the figure of the Great Detective, such narratives tend towards geometric patterns where the problem-solving aspect of the narrative predominates over the representation of a specific social and political context. Todorov notes the frequency with which the detective's accomplice functions as the narrator of the text, often depicted as composing the memoirs of his friend. This structure is evident in many of the Sherlock Holmes short stories, with Watson as the narrator-friend, such as 'The Speckled Band' (1892). In this story, Watson recounts how Holmes solves the mystery of the murder of a young woman, found inexplicably dead in her room days before her wedding. The murderer is her mercurial stepfather who uses the ingenious device of introducing a swamp adder into her room to poison her, thus preventing her from leaving the family home with her inheritance. Acting as an intermediary between the Great Detective and the ordinary reader, such narrator figures highlight yet further the formal construction of the whodunit as a retrospective narrative of logic and deduction.

---

[6] Ibid. 45.

In contrast, Todorov sees the thriller (or what he names *série noire* in deference to the French appropriation of the form) as a detective story in which the distinction between the story of the crime and the story of the investigation has become blurred. Created in America in the interwar years, its appeal was such that what would later be called the *roman noir* revolutionized the detective and crime fiction market. Narrative coincides with action and the story of the crime is largely suppressed in favour of an all-encompassing story of investigation. In the thriller, the detective-hero is no longer a genius of detection invulnerable to attack and far superior to his enemies. Rather, he is pitched into the very action of the novel, often disorientated and caught up in a whirlwind of events over which he has little control. The novels of Raymond Chandler are closely associated with this form of detective fiction. In *The Big Sleep* (1939), private eye and first-person narrator Philip Marlowe becomes embroiled in the affairs of the rich Sternwood family and a blackmail scandal. Drugged, beaten up, and threatened, Marlowe remains doggedly loyal to General Sternwood as a trail of corpses promises to divert him from his investigation. As Todorov notes, prospection replaces retrospection in such narratives, with the forward momentum of the narrative preventing any clear-cut comprehension of events. With no mediating narrator-figure to organize the sequence of events, the reader is aligned with the viewpoint of the detective-hero and shares his heady sense of confusion and danger.

Todorov recognizes that the innovation of the thriller comes less from the formal device of fusing the story of the crime and the story of the investigation than from the injection of a new and striking set of themes, characters, and settings. The urban context is the fitting backdrop for a cast of professional criminals, social outcasts, and corrupt lawmakers and judges. Violence, sordid crime, and amorality are described in a brutal and detached manner that often jettisons psychological introspection in favour of a gritty minimalism. The novels of Dashiell Hammett are some of the best examples of this behaviourist school of writing, refusing metaphorical flourishes and innuendos and adopting an objective style of narration that hints at the dark underside of human motivations. In *The Maltese Falcon* (1929), the reader follows the investigations of private eye Sam Spade into the whereabouts of a famed treasure, the Maltese Falcon, during which he encounters international art thieves, treacherous women, and hired gunmen. In fast-paced narratives interspersed with snappy dialogue and scenes of violence and murder, Dashiell Hammett offers the reader a dark and pessimistic vision of social reality with no time for sentiment or romance.

The third type of detective fiction outlined by Todorov, the suspense novel, retains the two-story structure of the whodunit but shifts the focus away from the reconstruction of the story of the crime towards the psychological terror of the main character. Often written from the point of view of a victim-protagonist, the suspense novel positions the reader to share the anxiety of the main protagonist, prey to unknown dangers. In terms of narrative sequence, Todorov notes that 'the reader is interested not only by what has happened but also by what will happen next',[7] constantly alert and fearful of future developments. This formula is worked into a devilish number of combinations in Sébastien Japrisot's *Un Piège pour Cendrillon* (1962) in which a young heiress, Mi, awakens after a horrific fire to find that her friend and companion, Do, has died. Yet as the story unfolds, the survivor suspects and comes to believe that she is in fact Do and has plotted to kill Mi for her money with the help of Mi's guardian Jeanne. Her fear and confusion colour the narrative and, after a police investigation, she is sent to prison but is still unsure (as is the reader) of her real identity. Todorov situates the suspense novel as a transitional form between the whodunit and the thriller, coexisting with the latter. He defines it as a hybrid type that gave rise to significant variations on previous conventions, such as the story-of-the-suspect-as-detective in which a character, wrongfully suspected of committing a crime, undertakes to prove his/her own innocence. With nightmarish scenes of inner turmoil, the suspense novel would feed the vogue for psychological thrillers popularized by such writers as P. D. James and Patricia Highsmith.

Todorov's structural description of detective fiction is influential for its recognition of the variations at the heart of what many had perceived to be formulaic genre fiction. His work stresses the evolution of detective fiction over time and the capacity of the genre to cast off well-worn codes and conventions and fashion a different combination of core elements. This acknowledgement of the protean possibilities of detective and crime fiction was an important step in validating the study of such popular fiction. However, other critics went one stage further in their examination of detective fiction and the *roman noir* more specifically. For if Todorov conceived of detective fiction as a body of writing ring-fenced by genre rules and expectations, others have inserted the *roman noir* into the wider context of twentieth-century literary history.

In her recent study of the 'noir thriller', Lee Horsley discusses *noir* as a 'popular expression of modernist pessimism'.[8] Although it has often been associated with the figure of the private eye, for Horsley the concept of *noir* far exceeds the limited cast of characters of certain crime novels and has formal and thematic affinities with forms of modernism. Indeed, for Horsley, the *noir* label has come to act as an organizing principle for a

---

[7] Ibid. 50.   [8] Lee Horsley, *The Noir Thriller* (Basingstoke: Palgrave, 2001), 1.

whole network of ideas and genres that reach into contemporary fiction and film and cross the barriers between high and popular culture. This is not to situate *noir* as a static literary mode or trend. On the contrary, its elastic qualities mean that it has shown itself to be a flexible and highly responsive form, remodelled over time by different writers. Yet certain narrative patterns and features do reoccur and Horsley concentrates on four in particular.

Firstly, Horsley emphasizes the importance of subjective viewpoints in *noir* fiction and film and reader identification with the first- or third-person narrators of the texts. The reader is kept close to the mindset of the main protagonist who struggles to make sense of the world around her or him. By creating unreliable narrators, *noir* fiction foregrounds questions of interpretation and plays with the notion that no one and nothing are as they seem. Secondly, *noir* narratives are centred on the presentation of ambiguous characters. Treachery and confusion blur the distinctions between detective, criminal, and victim. Characters' positions are un-stable and subject to sudden change and role reversals that problematize notions of individual guilt and innocence. Thirdly, *noir* narratives centre on the ill-fated relationship between the main protagonist and society. Characters are presented as doomed and isolated. They are unable to act independently or are cast out from their family and community and constrained by the prejudices and pressures specific to their historical context. Lastly, Horsley points to the socio-political critique inherent in much *noir* fiction. Writers who take up the *noir* model expose the violence and disorder that make up everyday lives. They challenge the record of the police and the judiciary to act as the moral arbiters of the nation and target the fears and anxieties of their readers.

As Horsley notes, *noir* narratives represent 'the damaged self' of differ-ent historical periods with their unsettling tales of social crisis and break-down.[9] Horsley's model could apply to a number of contemporary French *noir* writers, such as Jean-Bernard Pouy or Thierry Jonquet. Jonquet in particular plays with shifting identities, roles, and perspectives. In *Mygale* (1984), cosmetic surgeon Richard Lafargue slowly transforms the rapist of his daughter, Vincent Moreau, into a woman in revenge for his actions. As Vincent becomes Eve, the perpetrator begins to understand the terror of his victim and three different narrative perspectives open up a complex debate into the psychology of gender and social attitudes towards women and sexuality.

Although Todorov and Horsley come to examine the *roman noir* from very different perspectives—one as a structuralist, the other as a cultural

[9] Horsley, *The Noir Thriller*, 12.

historian—there are commonalities in their descriptions. They highlight the importance of setting and characterization and the relative lack of interest in the logic and problem-solving of earlier forms of detective fiction. Both underscore the moral ambiguity of the fictional worlds presented and the uneasy positioning of the reader who identifies with characters either on the margins of society or tipped into situations of chaos and despair. Dialogue and social interaction are the narrative motors of *noir* texts rather than description or psychological introspection. Yet, narrative models of *noir* fiction, as both acknowledge, are not fixed in time and evolve in relation to changing social and political structures. Culture and context are vital ingredients in assessing the impact and meaning of the *roman noir* for successive generations of readers.

Culture and context

In John Cawelti's model of 'formula fiction', detective fiction is described as having a cultural function that goes beyond the individual work.[10] Like other forms of popular fiction, detective fiction is defined as both a reflection of the preoccupations of a particular culture and as capable of influencing that culture's evolution. This dialectical relationship cannot be reduced to simple cause and effect as if literary forms could have a direct impact on human relations. Instead, the success of certain genres at different historical junctures is predicated on the ways they embody the prevalent concerns of the day. Detective fiction, like other forms of literary expression, draws on the collective fears and fantasies of its readers. It works in relation to a network of assumptions that not only constitute the basic values of a culture but also represent the dominant mood of an era, for example, the success of the spy thriller at the height of the Cold War. In this approach to detective and crime fiction, such texts operate at the crossroads of contemporary culture. They affirm existing attitudes by presenting a fictional world closely aligned with people's concerns, at the same time as managing change by periodically introducing new elements. Such a relationship allows tensions and ambiguities in a given culture to be resolved, both restating social rules and conventions and assimilating change. The emergence of American hard-boiled crime fiction can be examined from this perspective.

[10] John G. Cawelti, 'The Study of Literary Formulas', reproduced in Robin Winks, (ed.), *Detective Fiction: A Collection of Critical Essays* (Englewood Cliffs, NJ: Prentice Hall, 1980), 121–43.

The hard-boiled school of crime fiction developed in the pulp magazines of 1920s America, such as *Black Mask*, which drew themselves on themes and character types from the nineteenth-century dime novel. For later critics, this form of crime fiction developed partly as a response to the changing economic and social conditions of interwar America.[11] The Wall Street Crash and the Depression resulted in rampant unemployment, social deprivation, and mass migration as people flocked to the cities. In the wake of such momentous upheavals came the rise of gangsterism and organized crime, on scales previously unknown, in cities such as Chicago and New York. With Prohibition making bootleg alcohol and racketeering very profitable businesses, criminal elements seemed to be the only ones making the American Dream of rags to riches come true. In this context, a new narrative and idiom for stories of crime and detection was needed to mediate generalized feelings of unease, fear, and social breakdown.

The short stories and serialized novels of a writer such as Dashiell Hammett engaged in a realistic depiction of this America in crisis. Raymond Chandler, in his seminal essay 'The Simple Art of Murder', groups Hammett with a generation of American writers, such as Ernest Hemingway and John Steinbeck, who set out to enact 'a rather revolutionary debunking of both the language and material of fiction'.[12] For Chandler, the bourgeois novel of manners was no longer adequate to represent social change. Such transformations required innovations in both the style and subject matter of fiction. Hammett's contribution to this American revolution was his full-scale reworking of the staid, aristocratic atmosphere of the English whodunit. He catapulted the detective novel into the present, giving 'the authentic flavour of life as it is lived',[13] with his use of spoken dialogue and an understated prose style. Yet, perhaps the most striking feature of his work was the depiction of the 'mean streets' and his choice of a social milieu and cast of characters who were rarely represented in other fiction. In a famous turn of phrase, Chandler credits Hammett with writing detective fiction that 'took murder out of the Venetian vase and dropped it into the alley'.[14]

As 'formula fiction', Hammett's representation of interwar America draws on many of his readers' fears and fantasies about life in the big city. The pursuit of money, power, and advancement become the motivating forces for his characters. No one is exempt from a pervasive atmosphere of moral turpitude and decay, sometimes even the private eye is implicated.

---

[11] For example, see Robert Louit, 'Le Roman noir américain', *Magazine littéraire*, 20 (August 1968), 13–15, and Alain Lacombe, *Le Roman noir américain* (Paris: UGE, 1975).

[12] Raymond Chandler, 'The Simple Art of Murder', in *Pearls are a Nuisance* (Harmondsworth: Penguin Books, 1966), 181–99 (194).

[13] Ibid. 191.   [14] Ibid. 194.

This overwhelming sentiment of a society in disarray contaminates not only individual characters but also all levels of social and professional interaction. As Chandler described it, this is a world:

> in which hotels and apartments, houses and celebrated restaurants are owned by men who make their money out of brothels, in which a screen star can be the finger man for the mob, and the nice man down the hall is a boss of the numbers racket; a world where a judge with a cellar full of bootleg liquor can send a man to jail for having a pint in his pocket.[15]

Crime syndicates have taken over the city; prostitution, gambling, and money laundering are rife; those in power are corrupt and hypocritical, while the man on the street is the only one to pay for such widespread fraud and deception.

Hammett's vision of interwar America chimed with the concerns of his age and, as Lee Horsley has shown, the evolution of the 'noir thriller' since that period has kept pace with social change in America. Whilst the themes of social deprivation were prevalent in classic hard-boiled crime fiction up until the end of the Second World War, from 1945 until the early 1970s, the focus was more on exclusion and marginality, especially at the height of the Cold War when paranoia about the 'enemy within' inspired some American legislators to hunt out difference and suppress it. From the 1970s onwards, Horsley perceives dependency to be a key theme in *noir* fiction and film with satirical visions of consumer society as morally bankrupt and founded on excess and spectacle. As the twentieth century drew to a close, Horsley concluded that *noir* narratives had pervaded so many areas of American cultural production that they had become 'difficult to pin down'.[16]

Horsley's model of the social context and thematic changes in largely American *noir* cannot be easily grafted onto France. For while the classic hard-boiled novels of Hammett, Chandler, and others provide the narrative model, the *roman noir* has been appropriated by French writers to suit specifically French fears and concerns. More so than almost any other form of popular literature in France, the *roman noir* offers the opportunity to re-evaluate French national identity and cultural practice from the bottom up, from the perspective of writers and readers who perceive themselves to be marginal to the literary and political establishment. These 'eccentric' perspectives have given readers a cultural history of France in the form of a social investigation, an attempt to get the inside story on post-war economic and political reconstruction. The novels of writers such as Léo Malet, Jean-Patrick Manchette, and Didier Daeninckx denounce the illusion of a safe and carefully ordered social universe by

---

[15] Ibid. 197.   [16] Horsley, *The Noir Thriller*, 195.

depicting the random violence lurking beneath surface respectability and conformism. Indeed, as the century wears on, the French *roman noir* tends more and more to depict a dysfunctional society, denying readers comforting resolutions and, on occasion, encouraging a reassessment of their lives as complicit in the social disorder diagnosed by the text. Such writers and their creations have much to tell us about popular hopes and fears at specific junctures in French history, such as the Second World War or the events of May 1968, as well as the impact of shifting economic and social patterns, such as immigration and sexual equality. By presenting individual *roman noir* texts in dialogue with their historical and cultural context, this book will reassess how sources and cultural forms other than those of the accepted literary canon function as a significant focal point for important debates in post-war French society.

French detective and crime fiction

In *Southern Seas*, Manuel Vásquez Montalbán's hard-boiled Spanish private eye, Pepe Carvalho, stumbles upon an afternoon seminar devoted to the *roman noir*. In comic fashion, Montalbán sets out the many theories on the origins of such a form. Some speakers contend that the literary genealogy of the *roman noir* can be traced through Dostoevsky, Balzac, Henry James, Proust, Joyce, and other founding fathers of modern European literature. Others point to the American hard-boiled crime novel and the impact of the Great Depression, interpreting the *roman noir* as a response to the harsh realities of twentieth-century capitalism. The ideas come thick and fast but there is general consensus that 'the *roman noir* was invented by a French book-jacket designer who used the colour black for Gallimard's series of detective novels'.[17] This notion of the Série noire as a key moment in the history of the *roman noir* is not new. With its covers designed to look like an inverted funeral announcement (black background and white edges), it symbolizes the central motifs of the genre: murder and violent death. Yet Pepe Carvalho's rather drunken memories of the seminar throw up other issues and debates, such as the political and metaphysical affinities of the *roman noir* and its relationship to literary criticism. From nineteenth-century French realism to the American avant-garde, structuralism, and psychoanalysis, histories of the *roman noir* necessarily embrace divergent literary traditions depending on the viewpoint of the critic. For the purposes of this introduction, the *roman noir* will be situated in relation to traditions of French detective

---

[17] Manuel Vásquez Montalbán, *Southern Seas*, trans. Patrick Camiller (London: Serpent's Tail, 1986), 49.

and crime fiction. This is not to claim that such a socio-literary context gives a complete picture of the *roman noir*'s place in French culture. Rather, such a survey aims to identify a range of genre-specific influences that will have a bearing on the discussion to come.

Roman policier is the label most commonly used to designate detective or crime fiction in France. However, the term *policier* can be somewhat misleading as the police or representatives of law and order do not play as pivotal a role in French detective fiction as in Britain or America. From its inception, French detective and crime fiction has displayed an equal if not greater fascination with the figure of the criminal and the social climate in which her or his crimes are committed. Older fictional forms, such as the eighteenth-century gothic *roman noir* or stories of bandits and criminals with Robin Hood-style characters, appealed to the French reader of the day. One of the most influential of these early outlaw figures was Vidocq, a real-life character who made the transition from rogue informer to Head of the French Sûreté in 1811 at the age of 36. First published in 1828/9, Vidocq's memoirs caused a sensation. Widely admired in France and abroad, Vidocq and his escapades were to inspire some of the greatest French writers of the nineteenth century, most notably Balzac and Victor Hugo.

However, in terms of the detective format proper, the first recognizable narratives originated in America with Edgar Allan Poe's three 'tales of ratiocination': 'Murders in the Rue Morgue' (1841), 'The Mystery of Mary Rogêt' (1842), and 'The Purloined Letter' (1844). These short stories set out an investigative procedure and created an authoritative agent of detection, both of which had been largely missing from earlier literature dealing with crime. Poe's amateur detective, the Chevalier C. Auguste Dupin, wanders the streets of Paris at night like some vampiric lost soul alongside his awestruck companion, the narrator. He is the archetypal Great Detective, able to triumph over a bumbling police force and to decipher the story of the crime where others see only chaos. His methods of detection are a combination of empirical deduction (observation and assessment of material clues and evidence) and imaginative identification with the mindset of his criminal adversary. The three short stories also set out many of the narrative devices now common to detective and crime novels with their dark and murderous vision of the city at night. Translated into French in 1865 by Baudelaire, Poe's extraordinary tales won plaudits in France and elsewhere, with some readers struck by the 'French spirit' of the tales, seeing in them a marriage of French influences (Vidocq amongst others) and American form.[18]

---

[18] For a discussion of early French detective fiction and influences upon it, see Claude Aveline, 'Le Roman policier est-il un genre littéraire?', reprinted as a companion piece in *L'Œil du chat* (Paris: Mercure de France, 1970), 284–95.

Towards the second half of the nineteenth century, with rising literacy levels and the expansion of the cheap penny press, embryonic forms of the detective story emerged to titillate a diverse readership in France.[19] Emile Gaboriau produced the first French detective novel, *L'Affaire Lerouge* in 1863, adapting Poe's short-story structure to the exigencies of serial publication in the popular press. A tale of revenge, mistaken identities, and babies swapped at birth, *L'Affaire Lerouge* owes as much to French melodrama and adventure as it does to Poe's model of the cerebral detective. Yet these cliffhanger stories of vengeance and justice also introduced readers to two of the first French detective figures, the Père Tabaret and Inspector Lecoq. It was some years, however, before other French detective and crime writers made their mark on French popular culture.

Gaston Leroux and Maurice Le Blanc, both writing at the turn of the century, paved the way for later generations of French writers, establishing two influential detective fiction traditions. Leroux invented the character of Rouletabille, a teenage investigative reporter, and laid down many of the conventions that would be exploited in the whodunit: murder in a locked room, super-intelligent investigators, and their battle against master criminals in novels such as *Le Mystère de la chambre jaune* (1907). In a very different vein, Maurice Le Blanc carried on the French love for the criminal anti-hero with Arsène Lupin, the *gentleman-cambrioleur*, who pits his wits against the British and French police. Sensational twists and turns of the plot dependent on cunning disguises see Lupin fake his own death and join the Foreign Legion in one of his most famous escapades, *813* (1910).

After the First World War, French fiction, like that of America and Britain, entered the Golden Age of the whodunit.[20] In France, this type of detective fiction was best represented by the collection Le Masque, founded in 1928. Its success was largely dependent on translations of British and American novels, although French and Francophone novelists such as S. A. Steeman, and Jacques Decrest, certainly made their mark. Important writers began their careers at this time, such as the Belgian writer Georges Simenon who published his first Maigret novel, *Pietr le Letton*, in 1931. More generally, French detective fiction of these years was distinguished from its Anglophone counterparts by a greater emphasis on social context and an openness to mainstream literary influences. Established poets and novelists, such as Pierre Véry and Claude Aveline, published detective novels and brought a certain respectability to the form. Véry used poetic

---

[19] For an informative and accessible overview of early French detective fiction, see the opening chapters of Michel Lebrun and Jean-Pierre Schweighaeuser, *Le Guide du polar* (Paris: Syros, 1987).

[20] For an analysis of the whodunit in a French frame, see Pierre Boileau and Thomas Narcejac, 'Le lecteur contre le détective', in *Le Roman policier* (Paris: PUF, 1975), ch. 3, 49–62.

devices to introduce an element of the bizarre and supernatural into the whodunit formula, while Aveline injected a level of psychological realism into his series of novels featuring Inspector Frédéric Belot.

It was also during the interwar period that the American hard-boiled detective fiction first made tentative inroads into France. A number of Hammett's early detective stories were translated into French in the 1930s and published as adventure stories in mainstream collections. Although they attracted the praise of writers such as André Gide, these streetwise detective stories were not distinguished from a larger corpus of American literary exports during the interwar years. Banned during the Occupation, novels and films featuring the American criminal underworld and a crusading investigator were, however, still very much in public demand. Pastiche novels surfaced in collections, such as the populist Minuit collection, ghost-written by Frenchmen and depicting an imaginary America in sharp contrast to ration-obsessed wartime France. It was during these inauspicious years that Léo Malet published *120, rue de la Gare* (1943), providing the prototype for the French *roman noir* to come. Set in war-torn France with an ex-prisoner of war as its detective-hero, *120, rue de la Gare* was a story for its times and anticipated the wave of *romans noirs* to hit France at the Liberation.

In 1945, the prestigious Gallimard publishing house launched a new detective fiction collection, the Série noire. Its founder, Marcel Duhamel, a former surrealist turned translator, promised readers sensational crime stories and the collection opened up the French market to what became known as the *roman noir* in deference to the collection's black-and-white covers. After four years bereft of American culture, the Série noire filled its early lists with translations of American, and sometimes English, hard-boiled detective fiction. As Duhamel warned his readers in an editorial of 1948:

Que le lecteur non prévenu se méfie: les volumes de la Série Noire ne peuvent pas sans danger être mis entre toutes les mains. L'amateur d'énigmes à la Sherlock Holmes n'y trouvera pas souvent son compte. [. . .] On y voit des policiers plus corrompus que les malfaiteurs qu'ils poursuivent. Le détective sympathique ne résout pas toujours le mystère. Parfois, il n'y pas de mystère. Et quelques fois pas de détective de tout . . . Mais alors. Alors, il reste de l'action, de l'angoisse, de la violence.[21]

21 'The unsuspecting reader should beware: volumes in the Série noire cannot be safely given to all. The amateur reader of Sherlock Holmes style mystery stories will find little in them. [. . .] There are policemen who are more corrupt than the thieves they pursue. The friendly detective does not always solve the mystery. Sometimes there is no mystery. And sometimes no detective at all . . . But what remains is action, anguish and violence'. Reproduced in Franck Lhomeau, 'Les Débuts de la Série noire', *813*, 51 (1995), 5–17, 71–80 (79).

Duhamel promoted the *roman noir* as reading that was set to overturn the formal conventions of the whodunit, confronting the reader with a disturbing representation of social reality. Crime and disorder are endemic, whilst scenes of physical and mental anguish titillate the senses and draw a guilty complicity from the reader. The collection was dominated by translations well into the 1950s and early French writers were obliged to adopt American pseudonyms to fit the collection, such as Serge Arcouët (Terry Stewart) and Jean Meckert (John Amila). After a slow start, the Série noire increased the number of titles published dramatically, from two per year between 1945 and 1947 to two titles per month in 1948.[22] The populist reputation of the collection was established at this time and Gallimard imposed a uniform price and exploited wider distribution networks with Série noire titles available in railway station kiosks and corner shops, as well as in bookshops. Read widely by people from different backgrounds, the Série noire carved out an enviable position for itself as an icon of French popular culture, drawing admirers from the French existentialist movement, such as Sartre.

During the late 1940s and early 1950s a number of other detective fiction collections were created to imitate the publishing success of the Série noire. Prominent amongst these were Un mystère and Spécial Police, the latter credited with promoting the work of French writers, including some who had made their name in the Série noire, such as Terry Stewart (writing under the name of Serge Laforest). Yet due to the overwhelming influence of the American model, many critics have tended to dismiss early French *romans noirs* as either poor imitations or mere pastiche and parody of the American classics. It cannot be denied that some writers used the *roman noir* formula to make easy money by exploiting the latest fad or fashion. For others, however, the *roman noir* provided a template for a narrative that allowed them to represent a French context and French concerns. Série noire discoveries, such as Albert Simonin's *Touchez pas au grisbi* (1953) and Auguste Le Breton's *Du rififi chez les hommes* (1953), carry on the folklore image of the criminal anti-hero using modern-day gangsters. Set in big French cities, such as Paris and Marseille, these writers couched their novels in a dense local slang in order to recreate the atmosphere of the French criminal underworld.

Other French *roman noir* writers of the late 1940s and 1950s appropriated the form for more clearly politicized and trenchant critiques of French society. Novelists, such as Léo Malet, Jean Amila, and André Héléna, championed the cause of the oppressed and humiliated, often

---

[22] See Franck Lhomeau in 'Les Débuts de la Série noire' for a detailed overview of the origins and early development of the Série noire.

telling the story from their marginalized perspective. Their novels dealt with challenging topics in a tone of enraged despair at the human condition. Malet's *Le Soleil n'est pas pour nous* (1949) tackles male prostitution and vagrancy, while Héléna's *Le Bon Dieu s'en fout* (1949) begins in a penal colony in French Guyana to end in a bloody gun battle in small-town France.

The 1950s were also the decade when film adaptations of *roman noir* best-sellers made a powerful impact on French viewers. American classics *The Maltese Falcon* (1941), *Murder, My Sweet* (1944), and *Double Indemnity* (1944) were viewed as inaugurating a new filmic genre when they were first screened in France in the summer of 1946. The dark tone of the films and their pessimistic social vision led many to make connections with the criminal adventure stories of popular collections such as the Série noire. These American films created the legendary atmosphere of *film noir*, a world of danger, ambiguity, and panic in the big city. French film versions of Série noire novels were very popular with contemporary viewers and launched the careers of famous actors, such as Lino Ventura. However, for other French film directors, the American model needed to be adapted to suit French tastes. In *Les Diaboliques* (1955), Henri-Georges Clouzot rejects the stylized criminal underworld of American crime fiction. In this French *film noir*, the *noir* atmosphere is conveyed not through location but by exploring the psychological terror of the main protagonist, harried by inner demons and subject to forces beyond her control.

Over the 1960s, French detective fiction seemed to have lost its way. A few French authors of note made their mark, such as Pierre Siniac whose novel *Les Morfalous* (1968) debunks heroic myths of the French war effort in West Africa. Yet, this was all to change with the events of May 1968, a period credited with shaping the careers and political consciousness of a new generation of French *roman noir* writers. At this time, the term *polar* began to be used as an umbrella form for many types of detective fiction. An inversion of *roman policier*, in the *verlan* slang of the day, the term *polar* symbolized a young, confident, and self-conscious approach to writing the *roman noir*. At the head of this movement stood Jean-Patrick Manchette whose intellectual affinities with left-wing activism and popular protest made him the leading exponent of a new school of French detective fiction, known as the *néo-polar*.

The *néo-polar* revolutionized a moribund French detective fiction market by injecting radical political awareness into the classic American *roman noir*. Damning indictments of France as a consumer culture and 'society of spectacle' led to often nihilistic visions of individuals ground down by social conformity. Manchette coined the term himself as a derogatory term for an ersatz or imitation *roman noir* which could only repeat or rehearse the successful formula of the American original. This self-deprecating term, however, was widely used to describe highly politicized French detective fiction from the 1970s and early 1980s that denounced the institutions of the French State. In the novels of Manchette, A. D. G., Jean Vautrin, and others, the forces of law and order are depicted as little more than the flip side of organized crime. Politicians and statesmen are corrupt and repressive, whilst authority figures at all levels prove equally flawed and exploitative. Such a vision of contemporary France encouraged writers to move the action of their novels out of the big cities to the suburbs and the margins of society; to those places, such as public housing estates, perceived to be a wasteland for social outcasts and rejects. A substrata of characters emerge to people these images of a dysfunctional French society: the unemployed, the exiled, and the mentally disturbed. In the *néo-polar*, they represent the failure of a capitalist economy where those in charge refuse to acknowledge the human price of technological progress.

The success of the *néo-polar* of the 1970s and 1980s was an inspiration for many writers. The creation of hip publishing ventures, such as Sanguine and Engrenage, introduced readers to new French talent and reinvigorated the crime fiction market.[23] Film adaptations of the *néo-polar* made a considerable impact on the French film industry as the political thriller became a vehicle for discussion of the heritage and traditions of the Fifth Republic.[24] At the same time, specialist reviews were created to cater for reader demands for a more serious treatment of detective fiction, and annual festivals were organized for writers and fans to meet, the first taking place in Reims in 1979. The 1980s also witnessed the launch of influential new detective fiction collections, most significantly Rivages/noir in 1986 which became a serious rival to the Série noire. This collection took account of the intellectual prestige of the *polar* and republished (even retranslated) classic novels, as well as launching the work of a new generation of American writers in France, such as James Ellroy and Tony Hillerman.

By the mid-1980s, the radical political protest of the *néo-polar* had run its course but its effects were still felt in the work of writers whose novels presented a bleak image of contemporary France. The *roman noir engagé* (committed *roman noir*) as some labelled it, constructed an alternative

---

[23] See Jean-Pierre Schweighaeuser, ch. 7, 'Le néo-polar', in *Le Roman noir français* (Paris: PUF, 1984), 71–90, for a comprehensive overview of the collections, authors, and debates that fuelled the *néo-polar* phenomenon.

[24] For a full discussion of the political thriller during this period, see Jill Forbes, 'Hollywood-France: America as Influence and Intertext', in *The Cinema in France: After the New Wave* (Basingstoke: Macmillan, 1992), ch. 2.

social history of France designed to contest the dominant narratives of those in power.[25] The novels of writers such as Didier Daeninckx, Thierry Jonquet, and Daniel Pennac combine the conventions and themes of the *roman noir* with an acute sense of social responsibility. In *Meurtres pour mémoire* (1984) Daeninckx exposes the complicity of the French authorities in the deportation of Jews from France during the Second World War. This is not to say that these writers lack literary sophistication. Some of the most accomplished *roman noir* writers of the 1980s produced texts that were highly self-reflexive. They were a meditation not only on contemporary social issues but also on ways and means of interpreting that reality. In *La Bête et la Belle* (1985), Thierry Jonquet introduces a sense of the mythical and the fairytale into his narrative of a schoolteacher's descent into madness in suburban Paris. While Daniel Pennac in his Malaussène series of books, beginning with *Au bonheur des ogres* (1985), makes the act of storytelling one of the narrative motors of his fictional universe.

In more recent years, this image of the *roman noir* as the modern-day conscience of the nation has been encapsulated in the figure of Le Poulpe, a serial investigator invented by Jean-Bernard Pouy in 1995. Each of Le Poulpe's adventures is written by a different author and engages with polemical debates in contemporary France, such as right-wing extremism and the politics of abortion.[26] As a witness to his times, Le Poulpe signals the left-wing credentials of much contemporary French *roman noir* writing, campaigning, in an unorthodox manner, for social justice, tolerance, and the defence of democratic ideals. Today, his adventures can be read and composed on the internet in a move that aims deliberately to 'democratize' the writing process. Would-be writers are encouraged to submit the next chapter of an ongoing investigation to a reading committee which selects one for a final version for the web.[27]

So far, this overview of French detective and crime fiction has made no reference to women writers. France, unlike Great Britain and America, has not produced Queens of Crime in the mould of Agatha Christie or Mary Higgins Clark. Yet this is to overlook the sizeable corpus of crime writing by French women that has been largely marginalized by the critical establishment.[28] French women's relative invisibility can be attributed

---

[25] See articles in a special issue of *Les Temps modernes* devoted to the *roman noir*, 'Pas d'orchidées pour les TM', 595 (August–October 1997).

[26] See the first novel in the series, Pouy's *La Petite Ecuyère à cafté* (Paris: La Baleine, 1995).

[27] For the ongoing investigation, see www.membres.lycros.fr/lepoulpe/cadavres.html.

[28] Only four French women have won the prestigious Grand Prix de la Littérature Policière since its creation in 1948: Odette Sorenson, *La Parole est au mort* (1949), Laurence Oriol, *L'Interne de service* (1966), Madeleine Coudray, *Dénouement avant l'aube* (1978), and Brigitte Aubert, *La Mort des bois* (1997).

to a variety of factors, not least the difficulty of establishing the identity of women writers when in the past a good percentage used male pseudonyms to mask their gender. However, institutional factors have also played a role in their poor representation in critical histories of French crime fiction. The male bias of the detective fiction market, the macho reputation of some collections, and the lack of women commissioning editors have all militated against the successful insertion of French women into mainstream crime fiction. This situation has changed in the 1990s with French women writers infiltrating male bastions of French crime writing, such as the *roman noir*. Although many of these contemporary women writers reject the notion of a school of women's crime writing, it seems clear that a good number approach *noir* conventions and themes with a different sense of gender relations.[29] The novels of women writers such as Andréa H. Japp, Brigitte Aubert, and Maud Tabachnik, explore how female characters react differently to situations of violence and abuse. Japp's *La Femelle de l'espèce* (1996) centres on the character of Sarah Magnani and the kidnapping of her daughter. It highlights the failings of the patriarchal family unit. Brigitte Aubert's *La Mort des bois* (1996) has a tetraplegic woman, Élise Andrioli, as the detecting figure who uncovers the identity of a serial child-killer. While in *Un été pourri* (1994), Tabachnik sets up the prospect of female serial killer(s), murdering men who have committed sexual violence against women.

Into the twenty-first century, the French *roman noir* seems assured of an important place in the French cultural sphere. Conferences and publications signal its increasing acceptance by the academy, and authors once marginalized as *roman noir* writers have won general literary acclaim.[30] Established series, like the Série noire, have adapted to new audiences, changing the cover design and pricing to attract more highbrow readers, while new collections, such as Viviane Hamy's Chemins nocturnes, have introduced readers to an innovative generation of mainly women writers. Coupled with this diversification of outlets for the French *roman noir* is a respectful appreciation for the stylistic innovation of individual writers such as Maurice G. Dantec whose novels are an unusual hybrid of thriller and science fiction. The international fame of such writers as Daniel Pennac and Jean-Christophe Grangé has also assured France a place in the increasingly profitable publishing market of the 'europolar' with translations and big-budget films infiltrating the

[29] See Véronique Desnain, '"La Femelle de l'espèce": Women in Contemporary French Crime Fiction', *French Cultural Studies*, 12/2 (2001), 175–92, for an overview of recent French women crime writers and media responses to their work.

[30] Former *néo-polar* writer Jean Vautrin won the coveted Prix Goncourt in 1989 for his novel *Un grand pas vers le bon dieu*.

Anglophone world. As the boundaries separating high and popular culture begin to blur, the *roman noir* seems one of the forms best positioned to profit from a reconfigured literary landscape.

Choice of texts

Six *noir* narratives have been selected that represent some of the main developments and innovations of the *roman noir* in post-war French literature and film. Each chapter will focus on a particular decade and examine individual texts in relation to a set of political, social, or historical debates. This study is principally concerned with the *roman noir* but will include a chapter on *film noir* and references to film culture where appropriate. Although this book does not aim to provide a comparative analysis of *noir* fiction and film, it is important to recognize how the *noir* model has impacted on other media of representation besides literature. The focus of this study is also resolutely on the *roman noir* of popular culture, with each text having been initially published in a specialist *noir* collection, such as the Série noire. It is not the intention of this study to discuss the 'metaphysical' detective fiction of authors such as Alain Robbe-Grillet, Patrick Modiano, and others, who undermine or parody the traditional conventions of the *roman noir* and other detective fiction genres. The stylistic experimentation and deliberate 'defeats of detection' in these texts are symptomatic of critical trends in modern French fiction that go beyond the remit of this study.

The six texts and authors chosen have been selected partly for their formative influence on French *roman noir* traditions. Two of the texts are associated with turning points in the history of the genre. Léo Malet's *120, rue de la Gare* (1943) was the first French-authored *roman noir* to be set in a recognizably French reality. It illustrates the intersection of French and Anglo-American influences that marked the *roman noir*'s emergence into French literature. Jean-Patrick Manchette's *Le Petit Bleu de la côte ouest* (1976) is an important example of the *néo-polar* phenomenon when a generation of French writers appropriated the classic American model as a vehicle for a highly politicized, left-wing critique of French society. Some texts have been selected because they illustrate recurrent themes and preoccupations in the French *roman noir*, such as Didier Daeninckx's *Meurtres pour mémoire* (1984) and its emphasis on memories of the Second World War. Others are studied because they draw upon the *roman noir*'s vocation as a socio-political critique of its times, such as Daniel Pennac's *La Fée Carabine* (1987), while film adaptations and the intersection with *film noir* is the subject of the chapter focused on Henri-Georges Clouzot's *Les Diaboliques* (1955). Lastly, texts are discussed that challenge common assumptions and prejudices about *noir* narratives, such as Maud Tabachnik's *Un été pourri* (1994) which rewrites the *roman noir* from a feminist perspective.

I do not contend that the six *noir* narratives which make up this study represent the 'best' French *romans* and *films noirs*. Other authors and film-makers could have been chosen who would have given a different tonality to the study, such as Jean Amila whose committed writing made such an impact on a later generation of writers, or more recent authors, such as Maurice G. Dantec. The concern throughout has been to analyse interesting and challenging novels and films that have made both readers and students of the *roman noir* reflect on its myriad possibilities as a literary form and influential cultural narrative. Into the twenty-first century, the *roman noir* seems destined to infiltrate, even contaminate, the mainstream in exciting new ways. This study hopes to contribute to a wider re-evaluation of such a popular literary genre in French cultural history.

1 Origins and Beginnings:
Léo Malet, *120, rue de la Gare* (1943)

Je suis Nestor Burma, l'homme qui a mis le mystère knock-out.[1]

War and occupation

France's experience of occupation during the Second World War would scar a generation and a nation forced to submit to the exigencies of the German invader.[2] In May and June 1940, the French armed forces were defeated in four weeks. German blitzkrieg tactics of combined air and land assault overwhelmed the defensive Maginot line stretching across France's eastern border. Nearly two million French troops were captured, the vast majority of whom would spend the next four years in prisoner-of-war camps in Germany. Eight million refugees took to the roads in Northern and Eastern France in a mass exodus to escape the German advance.

With the defeat of France, the French Third Republic was ended and replaced by the Vichy regime under the leadership of a First World War hero, Philippe Pétain. The crushing conditions of the armistice imposed the division of France into various zones. The two main zones were the occupied zone to the north, overseen by German military authorities in Paris, and the unoccupied zone to the south, administered by the Vichy regime. This arrangement lasted until November 1942 when German forces invaded the whole of France. By the end of 1940, however, France was a nation divided not only along geographical lines but along political, socio-economic, and cultural lines too.

The Vichy regime was a dictatorial government founded on right-wing principles. Many of those involved in shaping its political and ideo-logical agenda were motivated by a desire to rid France of its Republican

---

[1] 'I am Nestor Burma, the man who dealt mystery a knock-out blow.' Léo Malet, *120, rue de la Gare* (Paris: SEPE, 1943). Further page references will be to the collection 10/18 edition (Paris: Fleuve noir, 1983), 79.

[2] For an accessible history of occupied France, see Henry Rousso, *Les Années noires: vivre sous l'occupation* (Paris: Gallimard, 1992).

heritage and to return to a nostalgic and highly reactionary image of a pre-industrialized France. This was best encapsulated in the Vichy motto 'famille travail patrie' (family, work, homeland) and the project of a 'National Revolution' aimed at regenerating what was perceived to be a moribund and defeated nation. Yet, what began as a form of forced coexistence with the German invader became a far more servile and compromised arrangement by the war's end. Vichy collaborated in the mass deportation of Jews from France to death camps in Eastern Europe and created ruthless military-style units, such as the Milice, to hunt down resisters and Jews. Policing and monitoring the French population reached into every area of public life, including the cultural sphere.

The occupation of France brought with it not only the loss of national sovereignty but also the loss of basic rights that French people had come to associate with living under a democracy, such as freedom of expression. The occupying authorities seized over two million books deemed to be either critical of Nazi Germany or counter to National Socialism. Over 850 writers and translators were banned, mostly due to their Jewish origins or left-wing affiliations. Many translations of British and American books were also banned, as well as a substantial number of school books. Even classical French authors and playwrights were censored if they were perceived to promote resistance to oppression. Censorship in this light was more than the control of mere information; it represented a sustained attack on French culture as the repository of values and ideals that could bolster national confidence during 'les années noires' as the war years came to be known.

It was during this dark time that the first French-authored *roman noir* was published. Léo Malet's *120, rue de la Gare* (1943) was a revelation to French readers introducing them to Nestor Burma, a Parisian private eye and recently repatriated prisoner of war investigating the past of an amnesiac fellow deportee in the winter of 1941. Burma's tale of theft, betrayal, and double—even triple—identities, invited the wartime reader into an exoticized version of their own lived reality of travel restrictions, food shortages, and an atmosphere of unspoken fear, tension, and dangers. Yet, the main innovation of Malet's novel is to create a *noir* universe that owes as much to a rich heritage of French literary traditions as to the hard-boiled crime writing of a novelist such as Dashiell Hammett. In *120, rue de la Gare*, plot elements from Hammett's *The Maltese Falcon* (1929) are combined with a rich network of French intertextual allusions to provide an implicit social critique of German occupation and its effects on everyday life. Predating the launch of the Série noire by two years, *120, rue de la Gare* is a prescient work for its use of the American hard-boiled formula to explore a period of crisis in French national identity.

Léo Malet: father of the French *roman noir*

Léo Malet's decision to write detective fiction was dictated by circum-stances. In April 1941 on his return to Paris from captivity as a prisoner of war, he was faced with the pressing need to make money in a depressed wartime economy. Malet's artistic and cultural allegiances as a pre-war anarchist and surrealist poet were a handicap in a country governed by the repressive and authoritarian Vichy regime. He had also spent much of his working life in shifting and unstable jobs on the fringes of the black economy. It was a friend from his surrealist past, Louis Chavance, later famous for the script of Henri-Georges Clouzot's film *Le Corbeau* (1943), who offered him the chance to publish pastiche American crime novels for reasonable sums of money. The German authorities had banned British and American detective fiction in July 1942 and smaller French publishing houses exploited this gap in the market, producing home-grown versions of a formula associated with American gangster movies of the 1930s.

Malet's first offering, *Johnny Metal* (1941), written under the pseud-onym of Frank Harding, was published in Ventrillard's Minuit collection. Malet created the character of Johnny Metal, a New York investigative journalist who infiltrates criminal gangs and drugs cartels bent on wiping out opposition to their economic interests in Mexico. In these *Johnny Metal* novels, Malet invents a fantasized America, drawing on clichés and stereotypes from popular culture. In classic hard-boiled tradition, Johnny moves through this urban landscape as an intermediary figure, an advo-cate of no particular group. His first-person narration aligns the reader with a jaundiced view of mid-century American capitalism, a phenom-enon despised and exploited by the main protagonist.

Johnny Metal demonstrates Malet's debt to Dashiell Hammett and the cold professionalism of his fictional private eyes, Sam Spade and the Continental Op. Hammett's books had been translated into French in the 1930s and published in series, such as Gallimard's 'Les chefs d'œuvre du roman d'aventures'. By the late 1940s, French critics such as Claude-Edmonde Magny were comparing the technical innovation of Hammett with that of Faulkner and Dos Passos.[3] These were writers whose objective style of narration and art of ellipsis (where more is inferred than stated) heralded a technical revolution for their French counterparts and their influence was discernible in work of writers such as Camus. For Magny, Hammett's contribution to this behaviourist school of writing comes

---

[3] Claude-Edmonde Magny, *L'Âge du roman américain* (Paris: Seuil, 1948).

from his development of a rigorous objectivism, which, like a film camera, records human interaction from the outside, replacing psychological introspection with an emphasis on appearance, actions, and gestures. By adopting the perspective of the private eye, charged with uncovering the dark underside of human relations, such techniques hint at the enigmatic depths of the most banal social interaction.

Nestor Burma, like Johnny Metal, shares many features with Hammett's individualistic detectives. Like his American brothers, Burma is a character who stands on the margins of society, able to straddle social classes and decipher the corruption and excesses of the big city. The plot structure of *120, rue de la Gare* owes much to *The Maltese Falcon* as, like Sam Spade, Burma seeks to avenge the death of his partner and is caught up in a chase for a hidden treasure. Unlike in Hammett's text, however, Malet chooses to position Burma as a first-person narrator, giving the reader access to his vision of a real and abstracted cityscape over which political, social, and economic interests vie for control. Burma's Paris of the 1940s and 1950s is a place where the collusion between establishment interests and the criminal underworld leads to injustices and a sharp divide between the rich and poor. As Jean-Noël Blanc styles it, Burma lives in 'la ville des pouvoirs' where lawyers, policemen, and gangsters join forces in pursuit of wealth and power, sacrificing decent Frenchmen along the way.[4]

If the *Johnny Metal* series gave Malet the opportunity to develop the *contestataire* perspective and prose style of his French investigator, the novellas written under the name of his grandfather, Omer Refreger, were to demonstrate the impact of surrealist poetry and imagery on his detective writing. 'Derrière l'usine à gaz' (1944) is of interest primarily for its representation of a city space and social order which draws heavily on surrealist motifs, such as dreams, eroticized violence, and evocative landscapes of gloom, fog, and terror in the city at night. In these narratives, inspired by another *roman noir* tradition, that of the eighteenth-century gothic novel, Malet creates a powerful sense of a deranged social order as the main protagonist, Sébastien Rossignol, is drugged, beaten, and haunted by fearful imaginings of horror and murder.

This sense of a fantastical social order has led Gérard Durozoi to read Malet's detective fiction as presenting an intermediary social space, poised between reality and the imagination.[5] With the eruption of unconscious impulses and intuitions into the everyday, Durozoi sets Malet's postwar detective fiction against a network of surrealist allusions, references,

---

[4] See Jean-Noël Blanc in *Polarville: images de la ville dans le roman policier* (Lyon: Presses Universitaires de Lyon, 1991) for a wide-ranging discussion of the city in mostly post-war French detective fiction.

[5] Gérard Durozoi, 'Esquisse pour un portrait anthume de Léo Malet en auteur de romans policiers', *Revue des sciences humaines*, 193 (January–March 1984), 169–78.

and motifs that undermine the moral and intellectual status of classic detective fiction, such as the whodunit. This poetic vision of the social is already evident in *120, rue de la Gare* as Malet presents the reader with an alternative reality to day-to-day life, knowable only through recourse to memory, chance, and the irrational processes of word association. In this first French *roman noir*, the detective solves the crime through a combination of logical deduction, brute force, and more intuitive methods. With Burma as the first-person narrator, the reader is invited to contemplate the fantastical possibilities of everyday life.

Malet's *120, rue de la Gare* functions, therefore, as a hybrid text, one that combines the socio-political critique of the hard-boiled tradition with European and French literary and cultural references. By setting a wartime story of crime, lost identity, and national recovery at this intersection of American and French *noir* traditions, Malet encourages the reader to interrogate the conditions of the Occupation in new ways. These privilege an image of France as a nation suffering from the imposition of a 'criminal' regime after its defeat by German forces.

120, rue de la Gare: facing an alien order

Malet's *120, rue de la Gare* begins in a German prisoner-of-war camp and with the arrival of an amnesiac deportee, known as La Globule. Registered and befriended by fellow prisoner Nestor Burma, La Globule's dying words, 'Dites à Hélène . . . 120, rue la Gare.' (tell Hélène . . . 120, rue de la Gare), are a key clue in the investigation to discover his real identity. On Burma's repatriation to France, some time later, the same words are repeated to him at Lyon's Perrache train station by his former partner, Bob Colomer, gunned down as he tries to catch Burma before his train pulls out of the station. These two scenes set in motion a series of incidents that lead Burma to criss-cross occupied France in pursuit of the mysterious Hélène and the location of 120, rue de la Gare. In a final Holmesian summation on Christmas Eve 1941, Burma reveals the betrayal and treachery that links Bob's death to the international jewel thief Jo Tour Eiffel, his daughter Hélène Parmentier, and a stash of hidden pearls.

In *120, rue de la Gare*, the Occupation emerges as a period of dislocation when the everyday is radically altered by the eruption of an alien order. Alongside the 'crime' story of stolen pearls and the murder of Burma's partner, there is the story of how France came to submit to the exigencies of German invasion. As Malet later commented in a collection of interviews, *La Vache enragée*, the blackout of the Occupation was the perfect counterpoint to the foggy city spaces of the whodunit and set the tone for a tale of the dark years of the war: 'ce noir absolu, voilà un décor dans lequel pouvait se dérouler un roman policier, plutôt qu'en plein soleil'.[6] For although Malet makes few references to the presence of the German occupier on French soil, his murder intrigue and the investigation of the detective are built around the consequences of invasion and the social inequalities it has brought with it.

The novel is peppered with allusions to shortages of all kinds: food, textiles, and alcohol. While the rich lawyer Julien Montbrison can smoke expensive Philip Morris cigarettes, Burma is constantly on the look out for tobacco. This is an important bartering commodity and is used by Burma to extract help and information from those lower down the social ladder. Indeed, being able to recognize the smell of rare imported cigarettes at this time of severe rationing helps Burma identify Bob's murderer. The weights and counters of the black market reflect the social upheavals of war as middle-class professionals—the cosmetic surgeon and the lawyer—are able to acquire real rather than ersatz products. They appear as a new aristocracy whose spending power extends to buying favours and influence with the French and German authorities, including covering up murder.

Such preferential treatment for consumer items extends to travel and the nighttime curfew that prohibited people from being on the streets at night without special authorization. Travel becomes a difficult and slow process for those who do not have a special pass or Ausweiss, often obtained through insider contacts. It is also a dangerous activity as the night skies are lit up by bombing raids and those out late risk meeting German and French patrols.[7] Yet such moments are also a privileged time for action when the fragile illusion of peace is broken and Burma and his associates, under the cover of darkness, are able to advance their investigations. It is during one such nighttime bombing raid that they discover the deserted house at 120, rue de la Gare and the body of a wounded woman pivotal to the unravelling of their investigation. Yet this remains an unusual event, one outside the normal order of things since, without a car, Burma's investigation is hampered by having to rely on others to organize and plan his movements, such as the sympathetic policeman Faroux.

Such travel restrictions have to be contextualized as part of a pervasive system of surveillance and social control used to subjugate an occupied people in *120, rue de la Gare*. On his return from the prisoner-of-war

---

[6] '[T]his complete darkness, now there's a setting in which a detective novel can unfold rather than full sunlight.' Quoted in Alfu, *Léo Malet: parcours d'une œuvre* (Amiens: Encrage, 1998), 18.

[7] In *Nestor Burma contre CQFD* (1945), the sequel to *120, rue de la Gare*, the noise and confusion of air raids proves the perfect cover for murder as gunshots are muffled by the planes flying overhead.

camp, Burma is hospitalized after attempting to save Bob's life at Perrache station. Yet, Burma exchanges one form of incarceration for another as he requires permission to leave the hospital and is even interrogated in the middle of the night as he lies in his bed recuperating after his ordeal. The hospital as a place of detention epitomizes the sense of overwhelming oppression in the early Lyon section of the book for Burma is under constant police surveillance. This official intervention in his life is pitted against the intimidation tactics of criminal elements who attempt to murder him and stop his investigation. However, the ultimate power to dictate his movements lies with faceless German bureaucrats. When he is ordered to leave Lyon for Paris as part of his repatriation home from the prisoner-of-war camp, he has no option but to comply.

Once in Paris, Burma faces a daily raft of obstacles in his personal life —from obtaining textile coupons for new clothes to heating his rooms. Even borrowing books from the library as research for his investigation is a trial. Novels by Sade have been removed from the shelves as undesirable reading, highlighting the moral crusade of the Vichy government. This censorship of the written word extends to spoken communication and dialogue as characters police their language avoiding compromising words or phrases for the occupier. It is part of Burma's opposition to such self-censorship that he deliberately plays with the subversive potential of language and its multiple meanings, presenting his own experiences of 'camp' life as an extended stay in a holiday camp. His constant use of English or American expressions, 'the right man', 'uppercut', and 'knock out' also signals his cultural 'resistance' to the xenophobia peddled by the collaborating Vichy government as it aimed to rid the nation of Anglo-Saxon influences.

However, it is true to say that resistance and collaboration operate as unspoken reference points in the text. Although Burma travels through Lyon, capital of the Resistance in unoccupied Southern France, to Paris, administrative capital of occupied France, Malet makes no reference to political figures or collective movements. Characters have no interest in political issues, whilst resistance activism is reduced to the level of a newspaper *fait divers* and is roundly rejected as a motivating factor in Bob's death by all, including Burma. A directly political history of the Occupation is eschewed by *120, rue de la Gare*. This is to be expected of a text published in 1943 in Paris when strict controls regulated every aspect of publication and would have prevented any openly anti-German statements. Yet, to a certain extent, Burma's lack of political involvement follows the model developed in Hammett's hard-boiled fiction. The tough detective in Hammett's novels is a character who functions alone in a hostile environment with few safe havens and a deep mistrust of interest groups and their motivations. Burma's suspicion of all those around him, including his devoted secretary-collaborator, Hélène Chatelain, is part of that same *noir* universe where betrayal and deceit seem to override friendship and loyalty. Yet, this is not to say that *120, rue de la Gare* cannot be read as deeply politicized text about the state of occupied France. As Theresa Bridgeman has speculated, Malet's wartime novels can be read as a 'countermove to the imposition of an alien order'.[8] In *120, rue de la Gare*, this is achieved less through appropriating the common tropes of American hard-boiled crime fiction than through the revelation of a 'social fantastic' which subverts the rational and political order of the Occupation.

As the individual consciousness through which events are filtered, Nestor Burma gives the reader a marginal and marginalized perspective on the Occupation. He operates alongside the official police investigation, often contravening laws in the process, and he refuses to endorse a wartime social disorder that rewards denunciation and betrayal. For Robin Waltz, Burma's status as an outsider is compounded by Malet's surrealist ploys that create a doubling of reality, a second critical perspective that can see beneath the surface banality of everyday life.[9] Burma embodies this privileged consciousness, able to decipher a fantastical other order of things. This allows him to solve the crime and to regain his bearings in an occupied France initially unfamiliar to him as a newly repatriated prisoner of war.

Malet's *120, rue de la Gare* has a number of features in common with the classic whodunit. The narrative begins with a body, that of La Globule, the amnesiac prisoner of war who dies apparently of a fever in an internment camp in Germany, and ends with a scene recapitulating events and identifying the criminals. In the last few pages of the novel, Burma gathers together all the major suspects on Christmas Eve 1941 to recount a barely disguised version of events. Burma sets a trap leading to the capture of the men responsible both for the torture of La Globule and the shooting of his partner Bob Colomer. To a certain extent, therefore, Burma conforms to the model of the Great Detective like Sherlock Holmes who uses his deductive powers to better the criminal and restore a conventional and conservative order.

However, the important breakthroughs in the investigation tend to owe less to the superior intellect of Burma than to a combination of brute force, intuition, and chance. Burma is ready to battle with his adversaries, sending one to a watery death in the Rhône as he is ambushed on a bridge

---

[8] Theresa Bridgeman, 'Paris-Polar in the Fog: Power of Place and Generic Space in Malet's *Brouillard au Pont Tolbiac*', *Australian Review of French Studies*, 35/1 (January–April 1998), 58–74 (62).

[9] Robin Waltz, 'Les Mystères de Léo Malet sous l'occupation', *Tapis-Franc: Revue du roman populaire*, 8 (1997), 116–27.

at night. Like his hard-boiled counterparts, Burma trusts appearances, facial expressions, and dialogue to gauge the reactions and secrets of his interlocutors. Burma is mistrustful of police procedures (and with reason, it turns out) and suspicious of ready-made solutions to Bob's death as a settling of scores between gangsters. Eventually, however, the mysterious identity of the amnesiac prisoner of war and Bob's murder are solved through recourse to dreams, wordplay, and free association, another fantastical order of things that Burma alone is able to interpret.

As in Malet's texts written under the pseudonym of Omer Refreger, the fictional universe of *120, rue de la Gare* is permeated with a poetic otherness that disrupts everyday life. The boundaries between the real and the imaginary are disturbed by the intrusion of dreams into the rational order of the detective story. Burma's intimation of the links between Bob Colomer and the amnesiac prisoner of war is prophetically revealed in a dream. As he lies in hospital, Burma elides the story of Bob's murder with a French cinema star, the notorious jewel thief Jo Tour Eiffel (aka La Globule), and the number 120, all of which lead to the discovery of the hidden treasure. Such unconscious processes of deduction are also projected onto the layout of the city as street names carry further clues for the investigation. Bob lives in Rue de la monnaie, hinting at the reasons for his murder, while Julien Montbrison, the corrupt lawyer at the heart of the intrigue, lives in Rue Alfred Jarry, an allusion to the grotesque figure of Ubu Roi, responsible for murder and mayhem in Jarry's Absurdist play. It would seem that the resolution of Bob's murder lies not in the deduction of the classic whodunit but in the possibilities of wordplay and free association.

The crime story culminates in a search for a hidden stash of pearls. Jo Tour Eiffel has given his daughter, Hélène, directions to the location of the pearls, disguised as a cryptogram: 'En venant du Lion, après avoir rencontré le divin et infernal marquis, c'est le livre le plus prodigieux de son œuvre.'[10] These directions are only intelligible to those readers familiar with the eighteenth-century gothic *roman noir* and able to apply such information to a detailed knowledge of Parisian geography. 'Le divin et infernal marquis' refers to Sade whose banned work, *Les 120 Journées de Sodome* is the clue to the whereabouts of the abandoned house where the pearls are hidden. Literary references are grafted onto precise locations as Sade becomes S.A.D.E., Société anonyme de distribution d'eaux, a building near the lonely house. Only those French insiders, such as Burma, capable of imaginative extensions can reach beyond the banal exterior of

---

[10] 'Coming from the Lion, after having met the divine and infernal marquis, it is the most prodigious book of all his works.' Malet, *120, rue de la Gare*, 95.

everyday life—a water company—to solve the cryptic puzzle and find the hidden treasure.

Burma's opposition to an alien order of German occupation is mediated, therefore, through the play of French language and French literary references. They form part of Burma's cultural resistance to Occupation, as transgressive and controversial French authors, such as Sade, trigger action and disrupt the monotony of the everyday. Yet other literary traditions come to play an important role too in the resolution of the mystery. In his wartime novel, *120, rue de la Gare* Malet reveals his debt to a wide-ranging history of detective fiction as a popular genre. It is in homage to the first Great Detective, Edgar Allan Poe's Chevalier C. Auguste Dupin, that Burma eventually solves the mystery of the hidden pearls as French and American literary traditions intersect for dramatic effect.

When the abandoned house at *120, rue de la Gare* is finally discovered by Burma and his associates, the pearls have already been stolen. Burma solves the mystery with a combination of deductive skill and imaginative intuition that is modelled on Poe's short story 'The Purloined Letter'. In this tale, Dupin is asked to find a compromising letter stolen from the Queen by the Minister D. who wishes to exploit it to his advantage. After fruitlessly searching his apartments, the police are baffled as to its location. Dupin solves the mystery by reasoning that the letter is hidden under the very nose of the police in Minister D.'s letter rack. This confounds the police who err by looking for complicated solutions when simplicity is best. Burma sees that his murderer has been inspired by Dupin's example. He discovers the pearls by looking in the most obvious location in the house, the mantelpiece of the main room: 'il [the murderer] songe à Edgar Poe et un trait l'illumine. *La Lettre volée* des *Histoires extraordinaires*, que tout semble désigner, vous en conviendrez, à marquer de son signe une telle aventure'.[11]

On rereading *120, rue de la Gare*, it becomes clear to one that Malet has scattered literary clues throughout the text to help identify Bob's killer. Montbrison is first introduced reading Poe's short stories, and later describes one of his employees as 'une perle', in an unconscious slip of the of tongue. For the alert reader, such intertextual references set Montbrison apart from the other suspects and confirm mistrust of a lawyer ready and willing to make a quick profit. Burma's ability to piece together such a story is a testimony to his reintegration into French life after the horrors of war and defeat. However, the narrative itself remains far more ambivalent

---

[11] 'He [the murderer] thinks of Edgar Poe in a flash of inspiration. *The Purloined Letter* from the *Extraordinary Tales* that, you would agree, everything seems to point to as leaving its mark on such an adventure', Malet, *120, rue de la Gare*, 193.

about the possibility of a similar process of recovery for the French nation as a whole.

Malet's *120, rue de la Gare* is the vehicle for exploring not only the consequences of crime but also the ongoing disruption of French national identity during the traumas of war. This sense of France having lost its way is symbolized by the multiple identities of the major characters in the texts, unable to fit their former lives to the new and unwelcome living conditions of occupied France. Burma is no exception, using the pseudonym Pierre Kiroul to disguise his past as a detective when he initially arrives in Lyon as a repatriated prisoner of war. At the beginning of the text, Burma's past as 'Dynamite Burma' is nothing more than a memory as he languishes in a prisoner-of-war camp at Sandbostel in Germany.[12] It represents an assured and autonomous pre-war identity that seems irrecoverable in 1941. At one level, therefore, *120, rue de la Gare* is about Burma's search to reassert his identity as a Frenchman able to overcome the humiliation of defeat at the hands of the Germans.

The prologue to the novel, 'Allemagne', encapsulates what would have been a common experience for a whole generation of Frenchmen during the Second World War: internment in a prisoner-of-war camp. Burma is no different from the other internees, undertaking administrative duties and concocting ruses to avoid being sent away on arduous and dangerous work teams. The prologue highlights the imposition of all things German by having the prisoners speak German as well as French. This is a sign of the reordering of daily experiences that prisoners accepted and exploited to survive. It is only with the death of La Globule, prisoner 60202, that Nestor Burma distinguishes himself from the mass of deportees, taking fingerprints from the body and having the cadaver photographed. In attempting to work out the meaning of La Globule's dying words, 'Dites à Hélène . . . 120, rue de la Gare,' Burma activates old ways of thinking deadened by the tedium of camp life but vital for his long-term survival.

The mysterious death of the amnesiac prisoner is the trigger for Burma's slow transition from subjugated internee to active participant in the world around him: 'Subitement je ne fus plus le Kriegsgefangen sur lequel les barbelés pesaient au point de lui enlever toute originalité, mais Nestor Burma, le vrai, le directeur de l'Agence Fiat Lux, Dynamite Burma.'[13] Like

---

[12] Autobiographical references make up an important part of the texture of *120, rue de la Gare*. Burma's wartime itinerary mirrors that of Malet, both interned at a prisoner-of-war camp in Sandbostel and having spent time in Lyon as itinerant young men. Malet also makes tongue-in-cheek references to people and places important in his own life, for example Bob Colomer clearly refers to André Colomer, a mentor figure for Malet in his youth as an anarchist activist.

[13] 'Suddenly, I was no longer the Kriegsgefangen so oppressed by the barbed wire fences that he was robbed of any originality, but Nestor Burma, the real thing, the head of the Agence Fiat Lux, Dynamite Burma.' Malet, *120, rue de la Gare*, 19.

the other French prisoners in Stalag XB, Burma begins as a KGF, the German term for prisoner of war, denied a French identity. Through his investigations, Burma rebuilds his confidence and reconnects with his famous past, as a much respected *privé*. Yet such an individual process is never divorced from a wider consideration of the effects of war on French society and French men in particular. Burma's investigation constantly brings the reader back to the memory of defeat and how it has marked a generation and a nation.

The rounding up of defeated soldiers as France capitulated in June 1940 is alluded to ironically by one journalist, Arthur Berger. He remembers how some soldiers attempted to avoid capture by exchanging their military uniforms for civilian clothes. Yet, this image of dishonour and collective shame has to be put alongside the fate of Burma's pre-war colleagues at the Agence Fiat Lux. Their life stories hint at the human tragedy behind Berger's mocking comments: 'J'ai appris que Roger Zavatter était lui aussi prisonnier; que moins chanceux, Jules Leblanc était mort et qu'enfin, tenant le milieu entre ces deux braves garçons, Louis Reboul avait perdu le bras droit dès les premiers engagements de la "drôle de guerre".'[14] Zavatter, Leblanc, and Reboul represent the experiences of a generation of Frenchmen traumatized physically and mentally by the Occupation. Burma's determination to solve the murder of another ordinary Frenchman, Bob Colomer, can be interpreted as a quest to avenge this series of broken lives, casualties of war.

The events of June 1940 are also central to the intrigue of the novel. The chaos of retreating French troops on 21 June 1940 is a cover for the torture of Jo Tour Eiffel, left for dead by his captors to be picked up in a confused state by the occupying forces. Jo Tour Eiffel is both the instigator of the crimes that lead up to Bob's murder and representative of the trials and tribulations of occupied France as a nation. Jo Tour Eiffel, aka Georges Parry (read for this 'Paris') stands in metonymically for the upheavals of war. A cultivated gangster of the Arsène Lupin variety from the 1930s, his downfall epitomizes the defeat of a nation and the negation of its glorious past. Left with no memory of his former self and subject to historical forces beyond his control, he dies at the hand of a fellow prisoner in revenge for past wrongs.

Yet, this too is a France where Frenchmen have contributed to their own afflictions. Germans and the German forces are totally extraneous to the murders and the search for hidden treasure. In *120, rue de la Gare*, it is

---

[14] 'I thus learnt that Roger Zavatter was also a prisoner, that Jules Leblanc, less fortunate, was dead, and that, finally, occupying the middle ground between these two courageous boys, Louis Reboul had lost his right arm in the first skirmishes of the "phoney war".' Malet, *120, rue de la Gare*, 116.

the richer characters, such as the cosmetic surgeon Dr Dorcières and the lawyer Montbrison, who are responsible for social disorder and betrayal. The novel depicts a social climate of fear and suspicion that is closer to the controversial depiction of small-town France in Chavance's *Le Corbeau* than to any patriotic image of France soon to rise from the ashes of defeat. Ultimately, *120, rue de la Gare* stages a pessimistic outcome to the war as those characters meant to provide help and leadership, such as the policeman Bernier, have their price and are ready to sacrifice others along the way.

If the collective fate of France and French manhood seems bleak, Nestor Burma symbolizes a far more successful transition to the conditions of war and the possibility of recovering past French glory. Burma as a detective figure embodies the contradictions and ambiguities of his age. As Steve Smith has persuasively argued, Burma's personal life history intersects with the wider social history around him, creating an opposition between 'the public discourse of legality and administration and the often conflicting private interests of the detective'.[15] In the context of the Occupation, Burma, as the French *privé*, zealously retains his French identity in the face of German and Vichy control and surveillance. His recuperation is mirrored in the journeys he takes across France. He begins as a repatriated prisoner forced to spend time in Lyon. Here, he is unable to function as his former self and is forced to rely on others to help him. He wears others' clothes, drinks and eats using their coupons, and sleeps on journalist Marc Covet's floor. His physical vulnerability is emphasized by his near fatal encounter on the Pont de la Boucle with an unknown assassin and he plays cat and mouse games with Inspector Bernier who tries to lead his investigation astray.

Once he arrives back in Paris, the investigation moves up a gear as Burma re-establishes his contacts and gains the confidence and admiration of former employees who plead with him to reopen the Agence Fiat Lux. In a reversal of fortune, Burma's recovery takes place as other lives, such as that of Jo Tour Eiffel, are lost. It is Burma's adaptability that makes him best suited to project himself into the post-war world as victor rather than victim. The finale of *120, rue de la Gare* is Burma's triumph of detection. This involves more than the capture of the criminals; it represents a victory over wartime prejudices that had dismissed a generation of Frenchmen as historical losers: 'Et ils étaient loin de se douter de ce qu'un K.G.F. affaibli (ils ont commis l'erreur de croire que j'étais revenu de

---

[15] Steve Smith, 'Between Detachment and Desire: Léo Malet's French *roman noir*', in Anne Mullen and Emer O'Beirne (eds.), *Crime Scenes: Detective Narratives in European Culture since 1945* (Amsterdam: Rodopi, 2000), 125–36 (130).

captivité entièrement gâteux) leur réservait.'[16] Burma's reassertion of his intellectual and physical dominance lives out a belief that French values and ideals would once again reign supreme. In this sense, *120, rue de la Gare* is a wartime narrative hopeful of national liberation and reconstruction.

The Série noire and the post-war *roman noir*

With the Liberation of France and the ousting of German forces in 1944 came a different kind of invasion: a flood of American goods, investment, and industrial advances.[17] America represented the land of prosperity after the penuries of war. It was a model for the future, promising the technological progress with which to rebuild a devastated French economy. Yet, the role of America in post-war French reconstruction could also be considered in a more ambiguous light. What would its impact be on a French national identity, already damaged by the experiences of defeat, occupation, and a bloody liberation?

A new wave of American hard-boiled detective fiction was emblematic of this 'coca-colonization' of France. Gallimard's Série noire, founded in 1945, realized the thrills and anxieties surrounding American cultural influence with its shocking tales of crime, violence, and gangsterism. With narratives saturated in despair and a profound cynicism about the human condition, the Série noire seemed well suited to a post-war France unsure of its future in a new world order.

There were hostile responses to this 'roman noir américain' from a number of quarters. Some French detective fiction writers understandably perceived such imported fiction to be a threat to their livelihood. André Piljean, later to write for the Série noire, argued that this invasion of all things American would swamp French culture as French translations of American originals became all the rage.[18] Other critics went further and condemned the vogue for American hard-boiled crime fiction as a pernicious influence on French literature as a whole. Thus, Thomas Narcejac

---

[16] 'And they were far from suspecting what a weakened K. G. F. (they made the mistake of believing that I had returned from captivity completely soft in the head) had in store for them.' Malet, *120, rue de la Gare*, 206.

[17] See Richard Kuisel, *Seducing the French: The Dilemma of Americanization* (Berkeley: University of California Press, 1993) for an insightful examination of French responses to American influence in political, economic, and cultural spheres.

[18] Piljean's objections to an American 'plan d'invasion' are cited in Deborah Hamilton, 'The Roman Noir and the Reconstruction of National Identity', in *Crime Scenes*, 228–40 (230).

proclaimed the Série noire to be the cultural equivalent of American factory production. It heralded the coming of a standardized model for detective fiction and the result would be a dumbed down, Americanized version of French culture:

> Dans l'usine à romans noirs, le téléphone sonne sans arrêt. Les machines à écrire crépitent. Aux murs, de grands tableaux noirs quadrillés de jaune permettent de voir d'un seul coup d'œil où en est chaque livre de la série, à quel stade il se trouve de la lecture, de la traduction, de la relecture, de la fabrication, du tirage, de la vente. C'est vraiment la littérature élevée à l'hauteur d'une industrie de chaîne.[19]

These fears of the American hard-boiled novel, and the Série noire in particular, as a corrosive influence on homegrown detective fiction were not without foundation. Translations of American and British novels dominated the crime fiction market in the late 1940s and early 1950s. With former surrealist turned translator Marcel Duhamel at the helm, the Série noire remained wedded to a core of American and British writers, such as Raymond Chandler, Peter Cheyney, and James Hadley Chase. Of the first hundred novels in the Série noire, only five were by French authors. Books sold better if 'traduit de l'américain' (translated from the American). In preparing texts for publication, Duhamel also operated an editorial policy that 'fitted' Anglo-American originals to a house style. Texts were cut and reconfigured to meet a required page length of 256 pages. Titles of novels were reworked in a provocative and allusive manner (Duhamel's creative affinities with surrealism coming into play) but sometimes in ways that had little to do with the English text. Translations were often freely adapted from the original and conformed to expectations of an 'American style' that masked the stylistic diversity of individual authors.[20] As Narcejac's nightmare vision suggested, the early novels of the Série noire were produced, packaged, and sold in a distinct fictional format.

The public appetite for the American hard-boiled formula was the subject of pastiche and parody. The publishing sensation of 1946 was *J'irai cracher sur vos tombes* (1946) supposedly written by Vernon Sullivan, a black American writer who, according to the preface, was unable to publish his novel in America because of its incendiary content. The novel was

---

[19] 'In the *romans noirs* factory, the telephone rings incessantly. Typewriters rattle. On the walls, big black charts criss-crossed with yellow show at a glance the progress of each book in the series, what stage of reading, translation, rereading, production, printing, and sales it has reached. It is really literature taken to the level of a production industry.' Thomas Narcejac, *La Fin d'un bluff: essai sur le roman policier noir américain* (Paris: Le Portulan, 1949), 164.

[20] Stephen Noreiko provides a detailed reading of the Série noire's early treatment of American originals in 'American Adaptations in the Série Noire: The Case of Chandler's *The Little Sister*', *French Cultural Studies*, 8 (1997), 257–72.

in fact the work of Boris Vian, dashed out in a fortnight in a bet with a friend. This novel, and three others written by Vian under the pseudonym of Sullivan in the late 1940s, were partly a mockery of French reader tastes for such Americanized mass culture. *J'irai cracher sur vos tombes* depicts an imagined America that panders to sensationalist images of racial tensions and social breakdown. It tells the story of Lee Anderson, a black American masquerading as white to avenge the death of his brother.[21] Lee's infiltration of a white middle-class suburban enclave ends in rape, murder, and a public lynching as he is punished for transgressing the laws and mores of American society.

On another level, *J'irai cracher sur vos tombes* could be read as drawing on wider Cold War paranoia about the 'enemy within'. Its obsession with racial origins reflects a general unease about shifting and unstable identities, anticipating the upheavals of European and French decolonization. Indeed, for mainstream French hard-boiled detective fiction writers of the 1940s and 1950s, this American model offered a privileged narrative for contesting social and political change in France. Although such writers focused on controversial and disturbing images of America, they adapted the hard-boiled genre for a transposed critique of their own culture. Strike action and labour politics, the conflict between corporate business and the local community, death row and capital punishment, are key issues in early French-authored Série noire novels.[22] In the work of 'pseudo-Americans', such as Terry Stewart (Serge Arcouët) and John Amila (Jean Meckert), the *roman noir* resonates with French domestic concerns over changing working conditions and the influence of global capital.

Throughout the late 1940s and early 1950s, a generation of French writers modified the American model to suit a French context, gradually setting the action of their novels not in an invented 'Amérique noire' but in an identifiable French reality.[23] The creation of the Série noire is often perceived to be the foundational moment in this emergence of the *roman noir* in French culture. Yet, as this chapter has shown, the narrative development and the meshing of French and American influences had already been conceived and successfully enacted two years earlier

---

[21] The irony of the fact that Vian was himself a white Frenchman masquerading as a black American writer has not been lost on critics.

[22] These themes are dealt with in Terry Stewart's *La Belle Vie* (1950) and John Amila's *Y a pas de bon dieu* (1950), and Terry Stewart's *La Mort et l'ange* (1948) respectively. For a reading of these novels as a critique of their times and home culture, see my 'Cultural Intersections: The American Hard-Boiled Detective Novel and Early French *Romans Noirs*', forthcoming in the *Modern Language Review*.

[23] It was not until the fifth Série noire title written by a Frenchman, André Piljean's *Passons la monnaie* (1951), that the action of French-authored fiction in this series took place in France. Piljean's novel was set during the Occupation and was a dark psychological portrait of a corrupt police inspector, Lomberger, on the trail of a counterfeit ring. It won the Grand Prix de Littérature Policière in 1952.

by Léo Malet with *120, rue de la Gare*. Malet set down the marker for a specifically French *roman noir* and knocked the whodunit from its pedestal as the prime detective fiction model for French authors.[24] His novel injected French literary traditions and a sense of French reality into an Americanized form, drawing on a left-leaning socio-political analysis that succeeding generations of French *roman noir* authors have admired.[25] But Malet's work did not provide the defining model for French *noir* fiction and film. The private eye would remain a peripheral figure in post-war French *noir* production, often rejected in favour of more ambivalent characters who transgress the boundaries of good and evil, criminality and justice. In films such as *Les Diaboliques*, the detective fails to solve the mystery in time as the tone is set for a troubling investigation into the public and private history of 1950s France.

---

[24] Although Malet was never published in the Série noire, critics of the day recognized his pioneering role, awarding him the first ever Grand Prix de Littérature Policière in 1948 for *Le Cinquième procédé*.

[25] Jean-Patrick Manchette has described him as 'le seul et unique auteur français de roman noirs' (the single and unique French author of romans noirs) in the immediate post-war era. Quoted in Alfu, *Léo Malet: parcours d'un œuvre*, 5.

2 Criminal Intentions:
Film Noir and *Les Diaboliques* (1955)

Film noir seems fundamentally *about* violations: vice, corruption, unrestrained desire, and, most fundamental of all, abrogation of the American dream's most basic promises—of hope, prosperity and safety from persecution.[1]

Cultural narratives of 1950s France

In the 1950s, France was undergoing a period of unprecedented economic expansion and modernization, financed in part by American investment. One of the most visible signs of this reconfiguration of the nation was the influx of American consumer products; from the 'belle américaine' (the luxurious American car) to domestic appliances, such as the refrigerator and washing machine. Integral to this process of equipping France for a new future was the American film industry, at once identified with the glamour of the United States and one of the main means of communicating the American Dream of wealth, free market economics, and liberal democracy to a European audience.

Yet, the exportation of the 'American Way of Life' into 1950s France was a process fraught with contradictions and ambiguities, as Kristin Ross has discussed in her study of the period, *Fast Cars, Clean Bodies*.[2] For if many people aspired to the American consumer ideal in the early 1950s (the stock of household appliances rose 400 per cent between 1949 and 1957),[3] France was a nation still struggling to survive in the austere conditions of post-war rationing and housing shortages. Images of polished kitchens and car ownership were an unobtainable dream for the majority in the aftermath of 'total war' and occupation.[4]

[1] J.-P. Telotte, *Voices in the Dark: The Narrative Patterns of Film Noir* (Illinois: University of Illinois Press, 1989), 2.
[2] Kristin Ross, *Fast Cars, Clean Bodies: Decolonization and the Reordering of French Culture* (Cambridge, Mass.: MIT, 1995).
[3] Cited in Richard Kuisel, *Seducing the French: The Dilemma of Americanization* (Berkeley: University of California Press, 1993), 105.
[4] In 1954, only 59% of French households had running water and only 28% had an indoor toilet. Cited in Ross, *Fast Cars, Clean Bodies*, 215.

In more sharply ideological terms, America, as an economic model to imitate, was also complicated by an image of the United States as an imperialist aggressor. In the early 1950s, a spectrum of left-wing politicians and intellectuals, especially the French Communists, denounced American culture for promoting an unforgiving and impersonal materialism. They highlighted the democratic abuses of Europe's wartime saviour, most famously the McCarthy witch-hunts of the late 1940s and early 1950s when high-profile personalities were tried for their left-wing and/or communist sympathies, blacklisted, and banned from working in the United States.[5] As the Cold War climate intensified, French society was simultaneously attracted and repulsed by American capitalism and the society it produced.

For Ross, France's hopes and fears for the future in the 1950s and 1960s were best exemplified by the nation's focus on domesticity and an idealized image of the couple as 'standard-bearer of the state-led modernization effort and as the bearer of all affective values too'.[6] France closed in on itself, retreating to the safe haven of the home, anxious neither to confront its recent wartime past nor the international tensions of the present. Ross's reading of the advertisements, films, and realist fiction of the 1950s and 1960s emphasizes how the home and the housewife came to represent this national desire to sweep away problems and make a new start. Such images were often couched in the discourse of cleanliness and order as if to symbolize a yearning for purity and a desire to erase unpleasant memories and fears. Yet, as Ross convincingly argues, this domestic ideal was in fact 'doubled' by another narrative of 1950s France, one that stood in sharp counterpoint to the apparently seamless process of modernization: France's wars of decolonization.

This 'dirty' story of French decolonization resurfaced most strikingly in the Algerian 'crisis', later dubbed 'la guerre sans nom' (the nameless war). Large-scale methods of arrest, torture, and murder were practised on the indigenous population of Algeria from 1954 onwards. These practises belied the image of a France cleansed by the trials of the Occupation. In often hastily improvised detention centres, 'clean' torture was perfected to leave no trace on the body using familiar objects found in bathrooms and kitchens as instruments of terror. Those in charge of interrogations used techniques developed by the Gestapo and French militia units during the Second World War, such as submerging detainees in the bathtub until

[5] A good number of those targeted were actors, film directors, and scriptwriters. Dashiell Hammett was imprisoned for six months in 1951 after refusing to provide the McCarthy hearings with the names of those who paid subscriptions to the benevolent fund of the New York Civil Rights Congress.   [6] Ross, *Fast Cars, Clean Bodies*, 126.

they lost consciousness. In a highly disturbing analogy, the domestic ideal and much vaunted purification of the nation after 'les années noires' of the Occupation had their sinister double in a repressed and censored history of decolonization.

In this context of rapid 'Americanization', how did the French film industry respond to the influx of Hollywood films which, like other American products, had been banned during the war years? Although other European nations, such as Britain, felt the full thrust of American cultural expansion, the French film industry seemed to have insulated itself fairly well against full American invasion during the 1950s. As Richard Kuisel notes, France maintained a 50 : 30 ratio in its favour during the decade, making French and Franco-Italian films some of the biggest box office successes of the period.[7] According to Kuisel, this achievement can be attributed partly to the domestic climate in which French films were made. The French government provided financial aid towards production costs and distribution so giving the French industry a much-needed boost after wartime disruption. Also, the 1946 Blum/Byrnes trade accords with America, which had initially enabled American films to flood the French market, were renegotiated in 1948 in order to cap American imports. Over the 1950s, Hollywood was limited to roughly 140 films a year.

However, it is not only the economics of the film industry that explain the continued predominance of French films in the 1950s. Viewer choices and tastes influenced and reflected cinematographic trends. During the 1950s, Richard Kuisel contends that French cinema audiences were characterized by 'a certain cultural conservatism'.[8] This meant that when the choice was open to them (and without widespread television, people were much less discriminating about what they saw on their regular trip to the cinema), French viewers opted for familiar French actors and directors, as well as tried and tested genres, such as costume dramas, literary adaptations, comedies, and detective films. With strict censorship laws in place, news references, documentaries, and films about France's colonial situation were effectively banned. Even if viewers had wished to look beyond the escapist films that they attended in droves, the political establishment of the day made this impossible.

Whilst the French film industry held up well against American competition in the box offices, American films had a huge influence on French film traditions in the 1950s. One of the most exciting developments for French film critics and directors was the advent of *film noir*. Made and

---

[7]   Richard Kuisel, 'The Fernandel Factor: The Rivalry Between the French and American Cinema in the 1950s', *Yale French Studies*, 98 (2000), 119–34 (120).   [8]   Kuisel, The Fernandel Factor', 127.

distributed by the American film industry, the concept of *film noir* was largely invented by a French film community who were the first to see these bleak 'criminal adventures' as a genre for their time.[9] For if *film noir* was a product of American capitalism, it also appeared to offer a stringent critique of that social and political order. In the midst of the Cold War, as France struggled to find its place in a new world order, the *contestataire* perspective associated with *film noir* seemed to speak to French fears and preoccupations.

Film noir and French adaptations

A pivotal year for the French film history was 1946. In that year, four films were shown in France that subsequently came to stand as some of the finest examples of what Nino Frank called 'noir' films: *The Maltese Falcon* (1941), *Double Indemnity* (1944), *Laura* (1944), and *Murder, My Sweet* (1944). Frank, writing in the left-wing film review *L'Écran français,* saw these films as providing a vision of the human condition that suited the age.[10] He linked their emergence in France to the prevalent vogue for hard-boiled crime fiction and it was largely in relation to such cynical and morally ambiguous narratives that he defined this 'new' film genre.

After the genteel whodunit films of the pre-war and wartime years, *film noir,* like the coming *roman noir,* represented a move away from the plot or enigma towards a focus on the motivations and psychology of criminal characters: 'the essential question is no longer "who-done-it?" but how does this protagonist act?'[11] Frank's early article highlights the originality of these films with their presentation of a 'third dimension' where facial expressions, gestures, and half-words communicate a sense of fear, anxiety, and unknown dangers. The lone figure of the private detective and the vampish heroine 'paying the full price' are singled out as representing a stable of duplicitous and troubling characters who embody the passions, repression, and amorality of the *noir* universe. Frank also praises the technical ability of *film noir* directors, especially the innovative use of first-person narrators in the form of voice-overs and flashbacks. He predicts that the French film industry must sit up and take note if they do not want their own film production to suffer from this explosive competition.

---

[9] Marc Vernet makes this point in 'Film Noir on the Edge of Doom', in Joan Copjec (ed.), *Shades of Noir* (London: Verso, 1999), 1–31 (1).

[10] Nino Frank, 'A New Kind of Police Drama: The Criminal Adventure', in Alain Silver and James Ursini (eds), *Film Noir: Reader 2* (New York: First Limelight Edition, 1999), 15–19.   [11] Ibid. 16.

Writing in the same year in the *Révue du cinéma*, Jean-Pierre Chartier's more muted response was representative of another strain of early criticism surrounding *film noir*.[12] For if he agreed with Frank's assessment of the innovation of these crime films, he laments the sexual obsession and depravity of many of the characters portrayed, particularly the cold and calculating women murderers in films such as *Double Indemnity* and *Murder, My Sweet*: 'these are monsters, criminals and psychopaths, without redemptive qualities who behave according to the preordained disposition to evil within themselves'.[13] He fears that depicting humanity as totally irredeemable is far too harsh a judgement and looks to a French interwar 'noir' tradition to inject some compassion and human decency into such depravity.

With the publication of Raymond Borde and Étienne Chaumeton's *Panorama du film noir américain* in 1955, the credentials of the American form were firmly established.[14] Borde and Chaumeton's study is a classic of its time in its penetrating analysis. It is coloured by the authors' appreciation of the surrealist themes of predilection of *film noir* directors: eroticized violence, cruelty, unrestrained desire, obsession, and death.[15] Borde and Chaumeton also analyse the emotional appeal of such films for cinema audiences: 'la vocation du film noir est de créer une malaise spécifique'.[16] In this, they emphasize the affective response *film noir* requires, cultivating in the viewer a heady sense of disorientation.

Borde and Chaumeton are also two of the first critics to identify the range of influences on American *film noir*, going beyond the commonplace comparison with the hard-boiled fiction of Hammett, Chandler, and others. They recognize the debt *film noir* owed to popularized images of psychoanalysis in its depiction of characters struggling with repressed desires or afflicted with traumatic memories. They trace too the impact of European film traditions, highlighting the contribution of French interwar poetic realism, in films such as Marcel Carné's *Quai des brumes* (1938), and the lessons provided by German Expressionism and its experimental use of lighting. Most importantly, they point out that some of the most prominent 'American' *film noir* directors were in fact German exiles who

---

[12] Jean-Pierre Chartier, 'Americans Also Make Noir Films', in *Film Noir: Reader 2*, 21–3.

[13] Chartier, 'Americans Also Make Noir Films', 23.

[14] Raymond Borde and Étienne Chaumeton, *Panorama du film noir américain* (Paris: Éditions de Minuit, 1955).

[15] See James Naremore, *More Than Night: Film Noir in Context* (Berkeley: University of California Press, 1998), 9–39, for a detailed analysis of how French philosophical and literary traditions shaped the reception of *film noir* in late 1940s France.

[16] '*Film noir*'s vocation is to create a specific unease,' Borde and Chaumeton, *Panorama du film noir américain*, 15.

had fled Europe to escape fascism, such as Otto Preminger, Billy Wilder, Fritz Lang, and Robert Sidomak. The techniques these émigré directors brought with them revolutionized black-and-white film production with their use of a moving camera rather than static locations, oddly angled and slanting shots, the play of light and shadow to create gothic effects, and the prevalence of reflective surfaces, such as water and mirrors. Such images have since become the hallmark of *film noir*.

Subsequent film critics, particularly in America, have taken up the lead offered by the French film community of the 1950s, discussing *film noir* along the lines of style and content. Yet, there is still much debate over what constitutes *film noir* and how to study it. Is *film noir* a historically distinct cycle of films, stretching from John Huston's *The Maltese Falcon* (1941) to Orson Wells' *A Touch of Evil* (1958)? Is it a genre with features that periodically resurface in later films, such as *The Usual Suspects* (1995) or *L.A. Confidential* (1997), and even cross-fertilizes with other film genres, such as science fiction in classic films such as *Blade Runner* (1982)?[17] Could *film noir* also be defined more generally as a style or look that encompasses literature, fashion, and other forms of popular culture?

These discussions aside, most critics, since the 1950s, have been in agreement that classic *film noir* is imprinted with the concerns of its age. In 1945, Lloyd Shearer could dismiss the view that the violence of *film noir* was connected in any meaningful way with the recent past.[18] With the benefit of hindsight, later critics have interpreted it as an important medium for understanding the social and political anxieties of the immediate post-war period. For critics such as Alain Silver and Elizabeth Ward, classical *film noir* of the 1940s and 1950s reflected American anxieties at the height of the Cold War, including the nuclear threat. With its images of a deranged world order, it was 'America's stylized image of itself, a true cultural reflection of the mental dysfunction of a nation in uncertain transition'.[19]

This image of disorder and breakdown resonated beyond America's borders. With countries such as France in the throes of massive economic

---

[17] See Marc Vernet, 'Film Noir on the Edge of Doom', for a full-scale attack on many of the current perceptions of *film noir*. In particular, Vernet challenges its chronological starting point (1941) and contends that *film noir* and its iconic figure, the private eye, are complicit with rather than critical of twentieth-century American capitalism.

[18] Lloyd Shearer, 'Crime Certainly Pays', in *Film Noir: Reader 2*, 9–13. Shearer was not prepared to accept that American newsreel footage depicting the atrocities of the concentration camps could have its fictional equivalent in the treatment of death and murder in *film noir*. Instead, he attributed the popularity of *film noir* to the economics of the Hollywood film industry and the success of a film such as *Double Indemnity*.

[19] Alain Silver and Elizabeth Ward, 'Introduction' to *Film Noir: An Encyclopedic Reference to the American Style* (London: Secker & Warburg, 1979), 6.

upheaval and with the horrors of wartime still fresh in people's memories, the *film noir* universe of isolation, alienation, and despair seemed extremely relevant to their situation. If we take a more global perspective on *film noir* as a cultural phenomenon, it can be examined as one American export that mediated not only its own national history but also the collective crises of an era.

In terms of *film noir* in France, a number of French film directors adapted the American model to suit French audiences in the 1950s. This took a variety of forms. At one end of the spectrum were adaptations of Série noire novels, heavily reliant on American hard-boiled character types and plot scenarios. As Jill Forbes has discussed, such French *film noir* or *film policier* often functioned as a pastiche or imitation of American *film noir*, for example *La Môme vert-de-gris* (1953), adapted from the Peter Cheyney novel of the same name and featuring the colourful secret agent Lemmy Caution.[20] Other film adaptations of the Série noire were more clearly focused on French concerns and cultural traditions. *Touchez pas au grisbi* (1954), taken from the Albert Simonin novel and starring Jean Gabin, is a nostalgic evocation of a French underworld culture. Max le Menteur, an ageing Parisian gangster, dreams of retiring with a stash of gold bullion but is dragged back into violent gang warfare when his best friend, Riton, is kidnapped and eventually killed by a band of young turks, headed by Angelo (Lino Ventura in his first film). Max's occasional interior monologues emphasize his tired awareness that the old ways and bonds of friendship are breaking down to be replaced by brute force. As Forbes notes, the contrast between two criminal orders in the film could also be read as a metaphor for the French film industry itself, fearful of American competition.[21]

Other French *films noirs* of the 1950s rejected the American locations and stylized criminal underworld of hard-boiled crime fiction. Instead, the focus of these films was on the psychological drama of *film noir*, presenting everyday characters harried by inner demons and subject to forces beyond their control.[22] *Les Diaboliques* (1955) sits firmly in this category. The setting is a boy's boarding school on the outskirts of Paris, governed by the tyrannical headmaster, Michel Delassalle. His wife Christina and his mistress Nicole, both teachers at the school, join forces to drown him in a bathtub and then dump the body in the school swimming pool. Their plans appear to go awry as the body goes missing.

---

[20] See Jill Forbes, 'Hollywood-France: America as Influence and Intertext', in *The Cinema in France: After the New Wave* (London: BFI, 1992).   [21] Forbes, *The Cinema in France*, 48.

[22] Interestingly, some critics of the day discussed *Les Diaboliques* as Série noire, even though it was not adapted from a Série noire novel. See Claude Mauriac, *Petite histoire du cinéma* (Paris: Éditions du Cerf, 1957).

Much of the film is given over to the mental turmoil of Christina, haunted by memories of her act and convinced that her husband will return to take his revenge. In the final scenes, the 'dead' Michel arises from a bathtub in the couple's apartment and Christina dies of a heart attack in shock. It transpires that Nicole and Michel have been in league throughout the film to provoke Christina's death and obtain her inheritance by faking Michel's murder. The adulterous couple do not win out, however, as a shadowy detective figure, the Commissaire Fichet, arrests them but intervenes too late to prevent Christina's death. Doubt and ambiguity still reign at the end of the film as one schoolboy claims he has spoken to Christina. Is he imagining this? Is she a ghostly presence or is she still alive and plotting her revenge?

Freely adapted from the novel by Pierre Boileau and Thomas Narcejac, *Celle qui n'était plus* (1952), the film met with mixed reviews. While many praised the virtuoso technical skills of the director Henri-Georges Clouzot,[23] others were appalled at the malevolence of the film and its representation of debased and depraved human relations: 'le monde décrit revêt l'apparence la plus sordide, la plus basse, la plus négative de l'humanité moderne'.[24] One explanation for such extreme reactions is suggested by Robin Buss in his study of French *film noir*. Buss suggests that the reputation of this film, and others like it, comes mainly from their setting and realism. For unlike Série noire adaptations, 'Crime, here, is not safely cordoned off in the underworld of the gangsters who feature so largely in American cinema: the milieu of these French films is not *the* Milieu, but an integral part of society.'[25] In *Les Diaboliques*, Clouzot demonstrates that the exoticized and scarcely credible 'Amérique noire' that French audiences were used to in novels and on their cinema screen could be transposed to their social reality. In the film, the 'clean' process of modernization has its flip side as women (and men) 'dirty' the domestic space of the bathroom with murder.

From novel to film: *Celle qui n'était plus*

The Boileau/Narcejac novel from which *Les Diaboliques* was adapted was not in fact a *roman noir*. Pierre Boileau and Thomas Narcejac were noted specialists of the suspense novel. Their productive collaboration began

[23] The film won the Prix Louis Delluc for the best French film of the year.

[24] '[T]he world described there takes on the most sordid, base and negative features of modern humanity.' Gilbert Salachas quoted in Philippe Pilard, *Henri-Georges Clouzot* (Paris: Seghers, 1969), 155.   [25] Robin Buss, *French Film Noir* (London: Marion Boyars, 1994), 27–8.

with *Celle qui n'était plus* (1952) and in this and other novels such as *D'entre les morts* (1954) and *Les Louves* (1955) the emphasis is on the slow mental dissolution of a character, overwhelmed by external events and a victim of repressed fears and desires. The conclusion of such narratives is often insanity, murder, or suicide as the main victim-protagonist fails to master the situation in which she or he is embroiled. The Boileau/ Narcejac novels were not intended as an analysis of a specific social milieu or as a political commentary on their times. Rather the dramatic charge of their narratives came from the detailed evocation of the inner anguish of a victim-protagonist.

Despite the abstracted and often psychologically complex nature of their texts, the early Boileau/Narcejac novels were highly sought after by film directors. Clouzot signed up the rights to *Celle qui n'était plus* just three days after its publication. This book had also attracted the attention of Alfred Hitchcock who later obtained the rights to their second collaboration, *D'entre les morts*, transposing the action to San Francisco to make the classic thriller *Vertigo*, starring James Stewart. Yet the adaptation of Boileau/Narcejac's work to a visual medium certainly posed difficulties for directors, as the authors themselves conceded in a 1980 interview.[26] How would directors recreate the intense interior monologues which were such a feature of their writing style? How would they find filmic equivalents for the abstracted metaphors of the texts?

Boileau and Narcejac expressed their admiration for Clouzot's script and direction of *Les Diaboliques*, although, as Christopher Lloyd has noted, this was tinged with some resentment at the lack of input they had into the final product.[27] As they commented in a preface to later editions of the text (retitled *Les Diaboliques* in deference to the film), 'le film de Clouzot est beaucoup moins une adaptation qu'une récréation'.[28] The original text differs from the film version in many respects. *Celle qui n'était plus* begins in foggy Nantes as Fernand Ravinel and his mistress, doctor Lucienne Mogard, plot the death of Ravinel's wife, Mireille. They aim to redeem her life insurance policy and move to the sunny climate of Antibes in the South of France.

After he drowns Mireille in the bathtub, things start to go badly wrong for Ravinel. The body is dumped in the stream at the end of the couple's garden on the outskirts of Paris and is intended to be discovered the next day as resulting from an accident. However, the body disappears. After

---

[26] See 'Entretien avec Boileau-Narcejac', *Cinématographique*, 63 (December 1980), 19–21.

[27] Christopher Lloyd, 'Eliminating the Detective: Boileau-Narcejac, Clouzot and *Les Diaboliques*', in Mullen and O'Beirne (eds), *Crime Scenes*, 37–47.

[28] 'Clouzot's film is much less an adaptation than a recreation'. Preface to Boileau/Narcejac, *Les Diaboliques* (Paris: Denoël, 1973), 7.

the fruitless attempts of a retired inspector, Désiré Merlin, to locate his wife, Ravinel becomes convinced that Mireille is a ghostly presence calling him from the dead. Letters and early morning visits to her brother seem to confirm that she has returned from the dead. Eventually terrified beyond all reason, Ravinel shoots himself. The narrative ends with an epilogue where it is clear that Mireille, indeed alive, and Lucienne are lovers who had plotted Ravinel's 'suicide' in order to redeem his life insurance policy and set up home together in Antibes. Yet, the 'diabolical' process of killing for gain seems to be about to recommence. The last lines of the novel hint at the scenario of Lucienne also ridding herself of the sickly Mireille.

The novel contained a number of disturbing features for the reader of 1950s France. The novel is narrated from the third-person perspective of Ravinel, thereby plunging the reader into his terror and incomprehension. Ravinel's profession as a travelling salesman who specializes in fishing tackle suggests that here is someone who is being reeled in, like a helpless fish, by the scheming women. The foggy scenes in Nantes operate as a pathetic fallacy indicating the extent to which Ravinel is handicapped by his inability to penetrate the murky designs of his wife and mistress. The book ends with the victory of the women protagonists, deviant monsters not only because of the crime they have committed but also as lesbians in 1950s France. In *Celle qui n'était plus*, justice does not win out (Inspector Désiré Merlin cannot conjure up the missing Mireille, as would his namesake), and sexual taboos have been transgressed at a fundamental level.

Clouzot's recreation of this narrative in *Les Diaboliques* differs in at least three major respects. Firstly, he redistributes the gender roles. In the film, it is the wife and mistress who plot to kill the husband, until the ending makes it clear that in fact the mistress and husband have been plotting murder all along. In place of foggy Nantes and a grey autumnal Paris is the boarding school, a claustrophobic and promiscuous environment in which the victim-protagonist, Christina, feels isolated and alone. Lastly, the ending is changed so that retired Commissaire Fichet captures his criminal duo but not before the death of Christina. Order seems restored at the end and the quotation from Barbey d'Aurevilly that opens the film and gives it its title seems fully justified: 'une peinture est toujours assez morale quand elle est tragique et qu'elle donne l'horreur des choses qu'elle retrace'.[29]

Yet the critical reactions to the film reveal that few were prepared to view the film as a morally edifying experience. On the contrary, reviewers

---

[29] 'A portrayal is always fairly moral when it is tragic and induces horror at the things that it relates.' For a complete transcript of *Les Diaboliques*, see *L'Avant-scène cinéma*, 463 (1997).

commented that the characters seemed to revel in their criminal activities, while the only character to show any remorse, Christina, is silenced by a heart attack at the film's end. The contradictions between what the film purported to show, what reviewers perceived, and how we might interpret the film today are crucial to an understanding of *Les Diaboliques* as a cultural narrative of its time.

Les Diaboliques: contesting the bourgeois order

Henri-Georges Clouzot was a film director who courted controversy. He began his career in the cinema as a scriptwriter during the Occupation, adapting detective novels by S. A. Steeman and Georges Simenon for the screen. His second film as a director, *Le Corbeau* (1943), transposed the real-life story of a series of poison pen letters in the town of Tulle in the 1930s to an occupation context. A small village tears itself apart as obscene letters are sent to individuals signed by 'the crow' (*le corbeau*) and denouncing their hypocritical behaviour. Shameful past histories are raked up, such as professional misconduct, abortion, and adultery, that could destroy the reputations and middle-class lives of many in the village. The film is saturated in an atmosphere of fear and paranoia that would have been highly evocative for an occupation audience under observation not only from German and French forces but also from neighbours and friends. Anonymous letters of denunciation were one common way Jews, resisters, and other 'undesirables' were identified by the wartime authorities.

Financed and distributed by the German film company, Continental, the film drew hostile reviews from all quarters. The right-wing moral majority under the collaborationist Vichy regime attacked the film for depicting an amoral picture of France that defied the family values and Catholic mores that it espoused. After the Liberation, Clouzot was accused of collaboration for working with a German film production company. In terms similar to the wartime moralizers, post-war critics attacked the film for its negative portrayal of France. This time it was perceived as having served the purposes of the Nazi propaganda machine with its image of a morally degenerate France. The film was banned and Clouzot was blacklisted from working in the French film industry. After two petitions signed by major intellectuals, the ban was lifted and Clouzot went back to fulltime cinema work in the late 1940s.

Le Corbeau established Clouzot's reputation as a provocative and unsettling director. *Les Diaboliques* was to carry on in this tradition with a *film noir* scenario that deliberately undermined some of the founding institutions of French bourgeois life: marriage and the school. In the discourse of post-war modernization, both of these were considered vital for the reconstruction of France. The school trained France's future citizens and inculcated Republican values, while the married couple constituted the nuclear unit (and active consumers) around which the nation was organized. In *Les Diaboliques,* they are the public (school) and private (couple) faces of a disturbed and hypocritical social order.

Michel Delassalle, authoritarian headmaster and homicidal husband, incarnates the gulf between the ideal and reality in both institutions. As the headmaster and patriarchal figure in the film, Michel rules the school with a rod of steel, humiliating his wife in public and ridiculing the other teachers. Any rebellion against this regime is met with physical or psychological violence and children, teachers, and his wife all evince fear in his presence. Yet Michel's arbitrary reign of terror and punishment has its parallel in other aspects of the school environment. The enclosed and introspective world of the boy's boarding school is no lost paradise. Clouzot portrays the schoolteachers as a group of social misfits who are no example to the children they teach. Monsieur Drain is an alcoholic and Nicole Horner, the mistress and fellow murderer, has been sacked from a previous job for undisclosed reasons. The young boys themselves are well versed in the vices and prejudices of their teachers as they smoke, make misogynist comments, and are constantly depicted as spying, voyeur-like, on the teachers around them. Moinet, the small boy who claims to see Michel when others believe him dead or disappeared, is revealed to be an inveterate liar. Like the little boy who cries wolf too often, when he does tell the truth no one believes him.

If the school environment is infected with a pervasive sense of moral corruption and duplicity, the institution of marriage is also seriously compromised. Idealized images of domestic bliss and companionship are replaced by a barren marriage, characterized by daily violence and aggression. In one of the opening scenes in the school dining hall, Michel attacks Christina off-screen in a scarcely disguised reference to marital rape. The sexual violation and exploitation of Christina is reflected in financial matters too as it is her money that pays for the running of the school, although Michel appropriates all the economic and symbolic power. Greed, avarice, and the need to dominate others are the prime motivations for murder in the film. Even the saviour figure of Commissaire Fichet who uncovers the crime and arrests the murderer is initially drawn to investigate by the lure of money.

However, women are by no means the victims of the film. Like many women characters in the *film noir* world, Christina and Nicole are presented as duplicitous and scheming, the archetypal black widow figures, killing their mate. For if the viewer feels initial sympathy for Christina and Nicole as an oppressed wife and a battered mistress (Nicole is shown in sunglasses in the first scenes because of a black eye inflicted by Michel), they plan and execute murder. Nicole is more fully the *femme fatale* figure who lies to and betrays Christina to fulfil her sexual desire for Michel. As a couple, these two characters function as a dialectical model for a series of tensions and fears around women in 1950s French society.

As in other Boileau/Narcejac novels, *D'entre les morts* in particular, the women characters in *Celle qui n'était plus* and *Les Diaboliques* can be read as personifications of France at a period of crisis. In Clouzot's reworking of the gender roles in the film, this perspective on the women characters is exacerbated for Christina and Nicole would seem to represent radically different visions of France at a time of modernization and economic change. Christina, as the wife and devout Catholic, symbolizes the values of a conservative world order. Her superstitions and fears form part of what was perceived to be dying French traditions and customs. Her belief in the sanctity of marriage prevents her from seeking divorce as a solution to domestic violence and she is raked by remorse at her actions, fatalist-ically accepting her persecution at the hands of Michel and Nicole as a form of divine punishment. As a woman, her status in the film is that of a minor and she is treated as such by Michel, deprived of her own inherit-ance and dominated in every respect.[30]

This presentation of women as minors within a highly patriarchal cul-ture is highlighted by Clouzot's decision to have the adolescent school-boys in the film act as a barometer of Christina's emotions and moods, for example the scene in the communal dining room when Christina refuses to eat her meal. The reaction of the children around her is to erupt into loud chants until they are led out of the canteen. Her individual rebellion is matched by their collective disorder and ill discipline. However, this empathetic link between the schoolboys and Christina is an ominous foreboding of the extent to which she, like them, will be unable to fathom the world of the adults and the plot of Nicole and Michel to bring about her death.

Christina's eventual rebellion against the old economic and sexual order is mirrored in an inverted form by Nicole, played by Simone Signoret. The modern emancipated woman, Nicole would seem to rep-resent the new opportunities open to women as the lifestyle models of

---

[30] Christina's representation in the film as a minor was certainly consistent with women's position in 1955 France. French women had to wait until 1965 before they had the legal right to manage their estate and assets without their husband's consent.

America clashed with conservative French traditions. As a single, sexually active woman, Nicole's affaire with Michel is a scandal in the school. As Christina's accomplice, there is also the suggestion of a lesbian bond so that Nicole seems to sabotage the conjugal unit from every angle.[31] Nicole is economically independent, having income from rooms she lets in her house in Niort, and she stands for the coming social and professional mobility for women. Her appearance—short hair, smart tailored dresses, sunglasses—and habits of smoking and drinking whisky give her a masculine air in sharp contrast to the flowing feminine dresses and long plaited hair of Véra Clouzot as Christina. The physical contrast between them underlines the oppositional models of womanhood they embody.

By the film's conclusion, the vampish and cold-blooded Nicole is exposed not as a threat to the patriarchal order of the school or French society but ultimately as a defender of that order in her pact with Michel. The challenge she posed is neutralized by the film's final twist and her arrest by Commissaire Fichet. Interpreting the film in the light of its ending, it would seem that it is Christina and not Nicole who offers the more sustained threat to the social order with her willingness to murder her husband for the benefits that would accrue to her. However, this reading of the film as reinforcing the status quo was not one many contemporary critics were prepared to endorse. The criminal intentions of the two women characters made far more powerful an impression than the restoration of order. It is by investigating some of the reasons for the disparity between the film's closure and its critical reception that we might come to reread the women characters in the film as representative of national as well as sexual uncertainties. With its subtextual references to a repressed history of decolonization, Les Diaboliques stands as a cultural narrative that negotiates troubling times.

Murder and decolonization

The second part of Les Diaboliques is given over to the viewpoint of Christina as victim-protagonist. The selective use of subjective camera shots means that the viewer shares her feelings of terror and remorse as, for example, she gazes down at the swimming pool waiting for Michel's body to resurface. In the textual play of Les Diaboliques, Christina is as much a victim of perception as she is a victim of the devilish plotting of

---

[31] As Michel confronts Christina at Nicole's house in Niort, Christina declares defiantly that the bed he sits on is 'le nôtre' (ours), L'Avant-scène cinéma, 46.

Nicole and Michel. The world around her comes to act as a reflection and intensification of her fears as if her psyche were projected onto the objects and people around her.[32] The spaces through which Christina moves become more and more restricted as the film progresses until she is confined to her bedroom and a series of narrow corridors in the last scenes of the film. It is as if space has collapsed in on her as her fears and guilt take over. However, this choice of Christina as the focalizer for much of the film does not result in unambiguous viewer identification with her plight. The play of good and evil is so blurred in *Les Diaboliques* that not even the battered wife can function as the moral centre of the intrigue.

This refusal to posit a moral centre could be attributed to the troubling presence of France's recent past and present in the film. Taking her cue from Kristin Ross's elaboration of a doubled narrative of 'clean' modernization as opposed to a 'dirty' narrative of decolonization, Susan Haywood interprets Michel's drowning in the bathtub as a reference to the Algerian war and French torture methods.[33] Writing in 1952, it would be scarcely credible that Boileau/Narcejac were themselves alluding to the Algerian war but more probably to the Second World War. They may even have had in mind the insurrectionary image of Charlotte Corday's assassination of French revolutionary Marat in his bath in 1793.[34] However, in 1955, Clouzot's intentions and targets were less ambiguous as the wars of decolonization would have been a value-laden reference for cinema audiences.[35] Indeed, if we were to take further Haywood's reading of this scene, the film itself could be re-examined as constructing a highly controversial narrative of French decolonization with women as its main protagonists.

On one level, *Les Diaboliques* is a film about rebellion against authority: schoolchildren against teachers, wives against husbands, women against men. In the fraught context of 1950s France, this could also be read as indigenous peoples against French colonizers. The school itself has all the appearance of a colonized land: a dictatorial leader who imposes order on the women and children by means of violence, deprivation, and psychological torture. In this context, the women characters appear as the oppressed and victimized whose rebellion is illusory and short-lived,

---

[32] J.-P. Telotte, in *Voices in the Dark*, describes these cinematographic techniques as typical of the subjective camera work of *film noir*, providing a 'language of heightened expression' and 'in effect turning the psyche inside out', 17.

[33] Susan Haywood, 'Simone Signoret (1921–1985)—The Body Political', *Women's Studies International Forum*, 23/6 (2000), 739–47 (744).

[34] I am grateful to Hanna Diamond for this insightful historical parallel.

[35] According to editorial notes in *L'Avant-scène cinéma* transcript of *Les Diaboliques*, Clouzot had wanted to make a film about the war in French Indo-China at this time but was prevented from doing so by strict censorship regulations (96).

partly because of the betrayal and complicity of one of them with the dominant order. They have few legal or civic rights in the face of persecution and torture.

Christina's eventual decision to rebel enables her to overcome years of social conditioning that have reinforced the rights of a colonizing and patriarchal power. Her marriage, like indeed the colonial image of a 'marriage' between France and its colonies, was one that obliged her to adapt to 'foreign' ways that stripped her of her inheritance and control of the school.[36] Michel's abuses of his conjugal rights certainly resonate with images of the colonial exploitation of indigenous people and their natural resources. Christina's pact with Nicole is, therefore, a bid for freedom, to rid both herself and the school of Michel's contaminating presence and to begin afresh.

The failure of this 'liberation' presages a pessimistic end to what would be a decade of violent conflict in Algeria and elsewhere. The bond between the oppressed and victimized (Christina and Nicole) unravels as incentives, pressures, and fear create divisions and splits. We could interpret this negative conclusion as suggestive of Clouzot's inherent conservatism in political and social affairs (tradition and strength win out). But it must be remembered that these images of rebellion, violation, and the disruption of established moral and social codes are precisely what viewers took away with them after watching the film. From our perspective too, nearly fifty years later, what remains is the audacious affront posed by the women characters in the name of freedom.

An American remake

Les Diaboliques has been remade three times in recent years, most notably as *Diabolique* (1996), directed by Jeremiah Chechik, starring Sharon Stone, Isabelle Adjani, Chazz Palminteri, and Kathy Bates. This big-budget version used the same setting and plot structure as the French original with Nicole (Sharon Stone) and Nia (Isabelle Adjani) plotting to murder Paul (Chazz Palminteri), the sadistic headmaster. However, the narrative is refashioned for the 1990s with a feminist twist. Instead of ending with the death of Nia/Christina, the concluding scenes of the 1996 film show Nicole appalled at the murder she is about to commit and attempting to save Nia. In a final struggle with Paul in the school's swimming pool,

---

[36] Clouzot cast his Brazilian wife, Véra Amado, in the role of Christina, thereby accentuating the 'foreignness' of Christina and the image of a marriage of cultures with the overbearing Michel.

Nicole is saved and Paul is killed by retired police detective Shirley Vogel (Kathy Bates) who intercedes to save both Nia and Nicole, advising them that they can mask the murder as legitimate defence.

As with the original film, *Diabolique* in the mid-1990s would seem to be writing its own cultural history of late twentieth-century America. *Diabolique* posits women not as a threat to the social order but as victims who fight back and reclaim their lives. The recasting of Commissaire Fichet as a divorced cancer patient whose husband has abandoned her signals *Diabolique*'s move away from the more stereotypical *film noir* roles for women as either vamp or innocent. In this film, it is women, abused and deceived by men, who take revenge in the name of natural justice, transgressing the law in the process. The women in their gilded cages, defined and conditioned by their relationship to men in the 1955 *Les Diaboliques*, have been set free by 1996. French crime fiction would have to wait until the 1990s for a wave of French women writers to do likewise for the *roman noir*.

3 Counter-Cultural Politics: Jean-Patrick Manchette, *Le Petit Bleu de la côte ouest* (1976)

Le polar, pour moi, c'était—c'est toujours—le roman d'intervention sociale très violent.[1]

Consumer society

Accompanying the accelerated pace of modernization in post-war France came the advent of a consumer culture that was to revolutionize urban living in the 1960s. National magazines, cinema, and increasingly television displayed and promoted the values of a consumerist culture, identified largely with home interiors, clothing, and popular entertainment. Yet as sociologists and cultural commentators noted, the consolidation of such aspirations and desires in France carried with it tensions and anxieties. How would a new generation of middle-class professionals ('les cadres') adapt to urban patterns of living that differed greatly from that of their working-class or petit bourgeois parents? Would the influx of cultural models from abroad, and America in particular, have a detrimental effect on national and regional traditions? Did the consumer abundance accompanying France's post-war economic miracle, known as *les trente glorieuses* (thirty glorious years), also bring with it a spiritual void?

Georges Perec's *Les Choses* (1965) evokes many of these debates in its dissection of the life of two twenty-somethings, Sylvie and Jerôme. They live in a small Parisian apartment depicted as an endless array of consumer objects on display. Theirs is a life consumed by the frenzied search for items that promise an elusive happiness. As contract workers in the embryonic world of market research, they spend their working lives listening to and recording comments on the latest baby food, the state of French agriculture, and what students need; consumer products, domestic affairs, and ethical debates all reduced to the same discursive level. Perec presents his two characters as a single unit in descriptive paragraphs that deny the reader access to their inner thoughts or even the

---

[1] 'For me, the polar was—and still is—the violent novel of social intervention.' Jean-Patrick Manchette, 'En guise de préface', *Chroniques* (Paris: Éditions Payot et Rivages, 1996), 9–17 (12).

differentiating possibility of dialogue. They are conditioned by their desire for success measured in terms of a materialist culture. For Perec, Sylvie and Jerôme remain throughout the hapless victims of an economic and social order that will only ever tease them with the illusion of fulfil-ment: 'L'ennemi était invisible. Ou, plutôt, il était en eux, il les avait pourris, gangrenés, ravagés. Ils étaient les dindons de la farce. De petits êtres dociles, les fidèles reflets d'un monde qui les narguait.'[2]

Sociologically inspired works, such as Jean Baudrillard's *La Société de consommation* (1970), examine the impact of such a consumerist culture on human relations. Baudrillard uses a structuralist framework to analyse the dominance of objects in contemporary French society: 'à proprement parler, les hommes de l'opulence ne sont plus tellement environnés, comme ils furent du tout temps, par d'autres hommes que par des objets'.[3] For Baudrillard, consumer objects have infiltrated the imagina-tion of ordinary French men and women to the extent that artificially stimulated needs and desires guide their lives. Consumers are condi-tioned to accept a sign system of values that ensure conformity and inte-gration into the capitalist system. Yet, Baudrillard picks up on the internal contradictions of such conspicuous consumption. Whilst it offers a cor-nucopia of plenty and infinite variety, it is built upon the exploitation and suffering of hidden others; those in the developing world who produce goods for a pittance. These countless others represent a sign system of oppression that many consumers are reluctant to acknowledge.[4]

The role of popular culture and the mass media in the consolidation of such a consumer society in France also interested cultural commentators in the 1960s. Edgar Morin in *L'Esprit du temps* (1962) examines the effects of a largely Americanized mass culture on French traditions. Morin recog-nizes that homogeneity and standardization were the hallmarks of this imported culture. However, in the realm of popular culture, Morin notes that the mass media are constantly attentive to the need to renew tried and tested formulas. The principles of repetition and conformism have as their dialectical opposite a search for creation and innovation, able to anticipate and satisfy public tastes. In the case of cinema, Morin points to the example of *film noir* in the 1950s and its effect as 'une électrode

---

[2] 'The enemy was invisible. Or rather it was within them. It had rotted, corrupted and ravaged them. They had been made fools of, little docile beings, faithful reflections of a world that scoffed at them.' Georges Perec, *Les Choses* (Paris: René Julliard, 1965), 69.

[3] 'Strictly speaking, men of wealth are no longer really surrounded, as they have been throughout time, by other men but by objects.' Jean Baudrillard, *La Société de consommation: ses mythes et ses structures* (Paris: SGPP, 1970), 17.

[4] In Simone de Beauvoir's *Les Belles Images* (1966), Laurence's existential dilemma is precisely not to be able to ignore the exploitation on which her comfortable middle-class life is built.

négative' (negative electrode) on the Hollywood film industry generating dynamic new models and ideas.[5] In the world of French detective fiction in the early 1970s, the *néo-polar* was just such an electric charge. It set the French *roman noir* on a different path for decades to come and finally distinguished it from its American counterpart.

May 1968 and the *néo-polar*

The 1960s had been a rather moribund decade for French detective fiction.[6] It had been dominated by stories of a stylized French underworld and violent gang warfare. A few innovative voices were, however, to be heard, such as those of Pierre Siniac and Francis Ryck who injected a more troubling sense of French social reality into their *romans noirs*. Also influential were *roman noir* writers who had made their name in the 1940s and 1950s, such as Jean Amila who continued his trenchant analysis of French history with such novels as *La Lune d'Omaha* (1964). Here, Amila casts a critical eye over the events of the Liberation in Normandy recounting the rivalries and secrets brought to the surface by the death of a French gardener at the American military cemetery near Omaha beach twenty years later.

The events of May 1968 were the catalyst for a new generation of French *roman noir* writers. Sparked by student protests at the Paris University at Nanterre, the events of May and June 1968 ignited a wave of popular protest amongst a younger generation. For many, they were rebelling against a decade of repressive morality and political conformism. For others, their actions had a wider significance. The militant left-wing critique that preceded and dominated the unfolding of events that year revealed a deep sense of disillusionment and anger at the state of Western democracy on the part of the demonstrators.

In her study of the cultural representations surrounding May 1968, Margaret Atack outlines the main features of a 'new politics' that animated the various *groupuscules* or left-wing groups operating outside the mainstream political parties of the Left.[7] Activists were committed to the destruction of capitalism and convinced that revolutionary action was

[5] Edgar Morin, *L'Esprit du temps: essai sur la culture de masse* (Paris: Grasset, 1962), 32.
[6] For a clear and well-argued history of the post-war French *roman noir* and its changing concerns, see Jean-Pierre Schweighaeuser, 'Du roman de voyou au roman engagé', *Les Temps modernes*, 595 (August–October, 1997), 100–121.
[7] Margaret Atack, *May 68 in Fiction and Film: Rethinking Society, Rethinking Representation* (Oxford: Oxford University Press, 1999), 5.

the only means of delivering radical change. America, as the banker of Western capitalist expansion, was perceived to be the epicentre of such global exploitation, using violence and intimidation to maintain its world dominance in countries such as Vietnam and Cuba. When applied to France, such an analysis highlighted how the French State was organized to maintain the power of the dominant bourgeois order, using the seductions of consumerism to keep ordinary people subjugated.

Some of the most prominent writers associated with the *néo-polar* were active or sympathetic towards dissident left-wing groups during the 1960s and early 1970s. Jean-François Vilar, Frédéric Farjardie, Thierry Jonquet, and Jean-Patrick Manchette all spent formative years campaigning on the political margins for a range of left-wing causes, most importantly Algerian independence.[8] Over a period of roughly fifteen years, from 1971 to 1985, such experiences of radical political activism would transform the possibilities for the French *roman noir*. For although the *néo-polar* phenomenon did not represent the majority of French *romans noirs* published during this period, it opened up new avenues for writers. France, not America, became the privileged terrain for such novelists. Collections such as the Série noire were given a new lease of life as young French writers chose to investigate their own social reality with inventive and highly politicized narratives.

The main targets of the *néo-polar* are the French State and the complacency of the dominant bourgeois order. The government of conservative President Valéry Giscard D'Estaing is repeatedly exposed as autocratic and self-perpetuating, relying on covert forms of oppression and violence to retain power. One of the major innovations of the *néo-polar* was to move away from the representation of crime as individual deviancy towards a sustained analysis of the State as a criminal institution. As Ernest Mandel notes, 'l'assassin, c'est le système'.[9] Manchette's second novel for the Série noire, *L'Affaire N'Gustro* (1971), set the tone for this form of political *roman noir*. The novel recounts in flashback the assassination of a Third World opposition leader in Paris by the ruling junta, aided and abetted by the French secret services and an unwitting small-time gangster, Henri Butron. This novel was read (and intended) as a

---

[8] In the early 1960s, Manchette was a member of the mainstream socialist party, Parti Socialiste Unifié (PSU), but also involved in the Union of Communist Students, and a dissident Communist group called La Voix communiste. Fajardie joined Gauche Proletarienne in the early 1970s and Vilar militated for the Ligue Communiste Révolutionnaire. Thierry Jonquet's early Trotskyist sympathies are clear in his choice of Ramon Mercader (Trotsky's assassin) as the pen-name for his first *romans noirs*.

[9] Ernest Mandel, *Meurtres exquis* (Montreuil: PEC La Brèche, 1986), ch. 17, 'Le "nouveau polar" et le nouveau roman noir français: "l'assassin, c'est le système".'

scarcely veiled fictional reworking of the Ben Barka affair when a leading Moroccan opposition figure was murdered in Paris in 1965 with the seeming complicity of the French authorities. In *L'Affaire N'Gustro*, international politics, state corruption, and the criminal underworld, all intermingle to give an uncompromising picture of France's place in a Cold War world order.

Alongside this vision of state crime and extortion, the *néo-polar* also investigates how such a model filtered down into bourgeois life. Doctors, lawyers, and middle-class professionals of every hue are presented as driven by a need to succeed that led them to eliminate those who stood in their way. Manchette's later novel, *Fatale* (1977), provides a bleak image of this social order from the perspective of a female professional assassin who is employed to kill off the business rivals and political opponents of rich French entrepreneurs. This notion of France as a social organism riven with conflict was largely responsible for the dark and nihilistic tone of the *néo-polar*. For underneath the veneer of convention, the *néo-polar* presents a social order ever ready to erupt into spectacular outbursts of violence.

If the themes of the *néo-polar* situated this new *roman noir* as largely left wing and politically radical,[10] it was also a disenchanted and disillusioned form of writing. As Jean-Pierre Deloux has noted, the *néo-polar* introduced a new set of characters into the *noir* genre who had little affinity with the iconic figure of the private eye and his moral crusade.[11] Here, characters are far more implicated in the social and political reality of their times: terrorists, former left-wing militants, the unemployed, disaffected youth, and, at the extreme end of social alienation, the mentally disturbed.[12] These characters are presented as both victims and perpetrators, often living in the suburbs or on large council estates and holding down dead-end jobs with little hope of change.[13] Caught up in a vicious cycle of violence and counter-violence, they are figures of social exclusion, the losers of society: 'Paumés, marginaux, marginalisés, chômeurs, laissés

---

[10] Not all writers associated with the *néo-polar* phenomenon were of the same generation or shared the same political beliefs. A.D.G., discovered at the same time as Manchette in the Série noire, rejected the left-wing heritage of the *néo-polar*. He proclaimed himself a monarchist in early interviews but later exhibited extreme right-wing views, writing for the Front National's newspaper, *Minute*.

[11] Jean-Pierre Deloux, 'Le Noir new-look', *Magazine littéraire*, 194 (April 1983), 21–3.

[12] For the use of a psychologically disturbed viewpoint on the contemporary world, see for example Thierry Jonquet, *La Bête et la Belle* (1985) and Manchette, *Ô Dingos, ô châteaux!* (1972).

[13] See Jean Vautrin's *Au bulletin rouges* (1973) where young factory workers act as *agents provocateurs* during national elections. The novel is a damning indictment of the indifference of those in power when faced with the social problems caused by the big council estates, a central feature of postwar urban planning.

pour compte de la société, révoltés, etc., tout les désigne à la fonction de bouc émissaire et de victime propitiatoire de la société qui les exclut.'[14] Their individual revolt invariably ends in failure as they are sacrificed in the name of collective (dis)order and conformity.

With the highly politicized themes of the *néo-polar* came a marked attention to questions of style and form, for if the content of the French *roman noir* was to change so too were the terms in which such a vision could be expressed. The stylistic experimentation of some of the most accomplished writers of the 1970s was a revelation for critics and readers. The *néo-polar* vogue exploded the hackneyed stereotypes and plot structures of the *roman noir*. Writers such as Manchette deliberately short-circuit the narrative closure and resolution of the *roman noir* and defy the pace of suspense and anticipation by playing knowingly with reader expectations. In his novels, sophisticated intertextual references to Flaubert, Marx, and Orwell jostle with erudite asides to American cinema, jazz, and crime fiction. The use of multiple narrative perspectives and the careful attention to metaphorical and symbolic layers of interpretation alerts the reader to the fictionality of his crime novels and their play on language and form.[15]

By the mid-1980s, the *néo-polar* seemed to have run its course. Belatedly consecrated by the French press as an important social and cultural phenomenon, some contested its originality. They claimed that earlier writers, such as Jean Amila, had paved the way and were not sufficiently acknowledged.[16] Others rejected the *néo-polar* label as a media invention that had served to group together indiscriminately a range of writers with different political and literary projects. For Patrick Raynal, current editor of the Série noire and *roman noir* author himself, the *néo-polar* was a 'mode aussi éphemère que ridicule'.[17] Yet despite the much-contested use of the term *néo-polar*, critics and writers agree that a wave of new authors in the 1970s revolutionized the form and content of the *roman noir* in France. As the writer most associated with this trend, Jean-Patrick Manchette stands out as a figure who united a radical social critique of contemporary France with a formidable reworking of *noir* style and form.

---

[14] 'Drop-outs, outsiders, the marginalized, the unemployed, those left behind by society, rebels etc, everything singles them out for the role of scapegoat and sacrificial victim of the society that excludes them.' Deloux, 'Le Noir new-look', 21.

[15] Jean-François Gérault's study of Manchette's life and writing, *Jean-Patrick Manchette* (Amiens: Encrage, 2002) addresses Manchette's literary techniques and contains some useful starting points.

[16] See Robert Deleuze, 'Petite histoire du roman noir français', *Les Temps modernes*, 595, 73.

[17] 'a fashion as ephemeral as it was ridiculous'. *Polar* hors série spécial Manchette (Paris: Éditions Payot et Rivages, 1999), 33.

Jean-Patrick Manchette: the reluctant founding father

The publication of Manchette's first solo novel *L'Affaire N'Gustro* in 1971 in the Série noire earned him plaudits as an exciting new talent. Manchette's foray into crime fiction was not, however, intended to lead to a glittering literary career. He began his working life in the 1960s on the periphery of the French film industry, writing résumés of other people's film scripts for production companies. At this time, he was involved in a number of small-budget films as a scriptwriter, mostly with Jean-Pierre Bastid with whom he would co-write his first published *roman noir*, *Laissez bronzer les cadavres* (1971). These early texts were written in anticipation of an eventual film adaptation.

Manchette's love of cinema was subsidized by work as a translator and he was the author of some thirty-five translations, mainly American crime fiction. He also translated *bandes dessinées*, and scripted original texts of his own. With the launch of his *roman noir* career in the early 1970s came a productive period as a crime fiction critic. His columns for the magazine, *Charlie mensuel*, and later for the journal *Polar*, constituted a much-respected analysis of classical and contemporary *romans noirs*. In sophisticated terms, he discussed the *roman noir* as a privileged narrative for understanding the workings of capitalist culture, inserting it into a social history of the twentieth century.[18] When he died in 1995, media tributes testified to the impact he had had on the French *roman noir*, crediting him with creating 'l'école du néo-polar'.[19]

However, Manchette's relationship to the *néo-polar* phenomenon was ambiguous to say the least. The author of nine novels published in the Série noire,[20] Manchette remained, until the end, highly critical of media investment in the *néo-polar* and was careful to distance himself from some of the excesses associated with it. He coined the term himself to designate a watered-down version of the classic American model which he much admired.[21] He was dismissive of writers who used the *roman noir* as a propagandist vehicle for dogmatic left-wing views and equally hostile to writers, such as Jean Vautrin, whom he believed cultivated literary pretensions that had little place in the *roman noir*.

[18] One virtuoso column, 'Novlangue de bois?' (1994), analysed American labour history from the War of Secession to the birth of the classic American *roman noir*, complete with full academic references. See *Chroniques*, 333–6.

[19] 'the néo-polar school'. François Guérif's obituary in *Le Monde*, 16 June 1996.

[20] One novel, *Fatale* (1977), was rejected by the Série noire and published in Gallimard's mainstream collection.   [21] See Manchette, *Chroniques*, 200, for his attack on the term *néo-polar*.

Jean-Patrick Manchette's vision of the *roman noir* owed much to a situ-
ationist analysis of cultural production. The situationists were one of many
groupings associated with May 1968. They developed from surrealist and
other art groups in the 1950s. In *La Société de spectacle*, Guy Debord, one
of the leading lights of the movement, defines contemporary society as
saturated in images and representations—'la société de spectacle'—that
mediate the individual's lived existence. Such representations are propa-
gated mainly through the mass media and a consumerist culture and are
designed to reinforce the power of the dominant élite and to enslave the
people. In thrall to illusory needs and desires, individuals live an alienated
existence. They are passive consumers, incapable of critical dialogue or
effective social action. The totalitarian control of such an order is such
that when new ideas or forces emerge they are recuperated for its purposes. Using an appropriately colonialist image, Debord describes the
'société de spectacle' as 'le soleil qui ne se couche jamais sur l'empire de la
passivité moderne'.[22]

For situationists such as Debord, literature and art are subsumed into
this 'société de spectacle' as 'culture-marchandise' (culture-goods), a
homogenized mass purged of any revolutionary potential for the reader
or artist. For Debord, the avant-garde artistic movements of the interwar
years, surrealism and Dadaism, represented the last phase of experimental art. With the defeat of Communism on an international scale in
the early twentieth century and the triumph of counter-revolutionary
forces (capitalism and eventually fascism) came the death of modern art
as a challenge to the establishment. With cultural production now at the
service of the dominant economic order, all that remains is to resist
from within, to use the cultural tools of the dominant order against itself.
This process is best served by a 'langage de la contradiction' (language of
contradiction) that defies critical norms in a spirit of excess, parody, and
subversion.[23]

Such theories on the history and aesthetic dilemma for contemporary
art were to have a profound influence on Manchette's attitude towards
the *roman noir*. Like the situationists, Manchette believed that modern
art could no longer have a radical mission and that all art was in fact a
product of and for the market. His choice of the *roman noir* was a deliberate one for he chose what he considered to be the most commercial
literary genre available for an attack on market forces: 'le ruse de roman
noir était de porter la critique et la rébellion en plein milieu de la

---

[22] 'the sun that never sets on the empire of modern passivity'. Guy Debord, *La Société de spectacle*
(Paris: Éditions Champ Libre, 1983), 13.   [23] Debord, *La Société de spectacle*, 158.

littérature la plus commerciale et vulgaire'.[24] In interview, Manchette repeatedly spoke of the *roman noir* as having an 'offensive' purpose, using military vocabulary to encapsulate his literary project as 'opérer derrière les lignes ennemies avec des romans noirs'.[25] His was a carefully planned guerrilla war against capitalism and the 'société de spectacle', conducted through one of its most valuable propagandist mediums, popular culture.

Yet Manchette was also aware that he was fighting on terrain that had already been prepared by the classic American *roman noir*. His admiration for Dashiell Hammett in his crime fiction columns demonstrated his awareness that they shared a sense of bitter disappointment at the failure of social movements to overthrow capitalism. For if the classic *roman noir* was created at a time when the forces of capitalism were in the ascendancy (interwar America), it also contained within it the seeds of a critical take on that culture: 'le polar est la grande littérature morale de notre époque'.[26] Manchette recognized that the behaviourist style of Hammett and others was a key weapon in the war on bourgeois culture and its literary counterpart, realism.[27] For their writing incited the reader to question the myths and conventions of character and psychology and to explode the 'lie' of social order: 'la particularité de Hammett et de quelques autres de ses contemporains [. . .] c'est de faire servir le style behavioriste à une démythification sociale. Ce ne sont pas les psychologies des individus qui sont "cacheés dans le livre"; ce sont les rapports sociaux; c'est le mensonge social qui maintient l'ordre'.[28]

From this perspective, Manchette's increasingly detailed attention to questions of style and form in his last three novels takes on special significance. In *Le Petit Bleu de la côte ouest* (1976), *Fatale* (1977), and *La Position du tireur couché* (1981), Manchette's textual subversion and experimentation is an integral part of his social critique. As he commented in interview, his *gauchiste* themes and polemics were accompanied by a desire to elevate his novels to the level of a 'méta-polar', a

---

[24] 'The roman noir's trick was to bring criticism and rebellion into the very heart of the most commercial and popular literature.' Jean Patrick Manchette writing about Léo Malet in *Polar* spécial Manchette (1999), 171.

[25] 'operating behind enemy lines with *romans noirs*'. Interview, 'Jean-Patrick Manchette, la position du romancier noir solitaire', *Combo* (Autumn, 1991), 7–14 (8).

[26] 'the polar is the great moral literature of our era'. Manchette, *Chroniques*, 31.

[27] See Franck Frommer, 'Jean-Patrick Manchette: le facteur fatal', in *Mouvements*, 15/16 (May–August 2001), 88–95, for an excellent analysis of Manchette's writing as a critical deconstruction of realism.

[28] 'the distinctive feature of Hammett and some of his contemporaries ... is to use the behaviourist style for the purposes of a social demythification. It is not individual psychologies that are "hidden in the book"; it is social relations; it is the social lie that maintains order.' Manchette, *Chroniques*, 313.

reflection on the form and possibilities of the *roman noir* as *littérature contestataire*.[29]

Le Petit Bleu de la côte ouest: 'tourner en rond'

Le Petit Bleu tells the story of Georges Gerfaut, a marketing manager for a large American multinational corporation. Whilst driving his Mercedes late one night on the Parisian *périphérique*, he picks up a man who has been shot by two contract killers, Bastien and Carlo. They are in the pay of a reclusive former secret service chief from the Dominican Republic, Alonso Emerich y Emerich, living under an assumed name in France. A desperate manhunt then ensues across France as Bastien and Carlo attempt to kill Georges for his unwitting part in the botched contract killing. Scenes of tragi-comic proportions take place in the seaside resort of Saint-Georges-de-Didonne as the killers try to drown an uncomprehending Georges amid holiday bathers. Cars later erupt into flames as shots are exchanged at a petrol station and Bastien is burnt alive. After a frantic trek through dense forest, Georges eventually recovers at the home of Corporal Raguse in an isolated village in the Alps and drifts into a new identity as the Corporal's friend and helper, Georges Sorel.[30] However, his past catches up with him and he is nearly gunned down by the enraged Carlo, out to avenge his partner's death. In the last chapters of the book, Georges tracks down Emerich y Emerich, kills him, and returns to his old life. The story ends with Georges aimlessly driving around the Parisian *pérphérique* almost exactly as he was presented in the first pages of the novel.

According to Manchette, *Le Petit Bleu* was written as 'un truc sur la malaise des cadres'.[31] The title is richly evocative. 'Le petit bleu' is both a jazz ballad and an intimation of Georges's own twentieth-century 'blues' as an individual alienated by the materialist dreams of his age. It can also be contrasted to 'le grand bleu', an image of the sea and the expansive freedom that Georges lacks. A former left-wing militant with the PSU (like Manchette), Georges and his wife Béa represent a possible future for Perec's couple in *Les Choses*. They have all the comforts of a solid

---

[29] Interview with Manchette, 'Réponses', *Littérature*, 49 (February, 1983), 102–7 (103–4).
[30] Georges Sorel was an early twentieth-century trade union activist who advocated violence as a force for social change. Sorel could also be an intertextual play on Julien Sorel, hero of Stendhal's *Le Rouge et le noir* (1830), another non-conformist who failed to make his mark.
[31] 'a thing about executive unease'. Interview, 'Le Roman noir reprend des couleurs', *Nouvelles Littéraires*, (1982), 44–5 (45).

bourgeois life and work in marketing and public relations (Béa is a press attachée). In a manner reminiscent of Perec's novel, Manchette describes their home as a succession of objects that define their values and identity:

> Gerfaut fumait et regardait le living, dont une partie seulement du système d'éclairage, la plus discrète, donnait actuellement de la lumière. De sorte qu'une pénombre élégante baignait les fauteuils assortis au canapé, et la table à café, et les cubes de plastique blanc cassé où reposaient un coffret à cigarettes, une lampe en forme de champignon en plastique vermillon, les numéros récents de *L'Express, Le Point, Le Nouvel Observateur, Le Monde, Playboy* en édition américaine, *L'Écho des Savanes* et d'autres publications; et les casiers à disques où l'on trouvait des disques de musique symphonique et d'opéra et de jazz *west coast* pour une valeur de quatre ou cinq mille francs.[32]

The careful lighting picks up the studied elegance of the room. All items of furniture are described by their form, the material from which they are made, and their position in the room. They are given the weight and status of a living thing. No object is out of place and the magazines on the coffee table suggest the popular intellectualism of the couple (*Playboy* in its American version being a mark of libertine and cosmopolitan views) The range of music indicates the informed tastes of the listeners while the west coast jazz (deliberately italicized in American) runs as a leitmotif through the novel, situating Georges as a figure who has assimilated American, and therefore consumerist, values. Financial value counts as a marker of worth and, in this list-like enumeration of objects, the reader is encouraged to survey, like Georges, the impressive extent of his domain.

Manchette's attention to brands and makes in the novel mocks the excesses of consumer culture. Cars are never just that but a Mercedes, Ford Taunus, or a Lancia Beta Berline 1800. Lighters are a Criquet, cigarettes are a Gitane-filtre, and there is a running play on brands of whisky to the extent that drinking Cutty Sark or Glenlivet constitutes an important personality feature when compared to 4 Roses bourbon. The detailed reference to makes of guns, their calibre, shooting distances, and effects on the human body are, thereby, contextualized as another fetishized object in a consumerist culture.

---

[32] 'Gerfaut smoked on and looked at the living room, at present lit up only by the room's most subdued lighting, so that an elegant half shadow bathed the armchairs matching the sofa, and the coffee table, and the off-white plastic cubes on which were placed a cigarette box, a scarlet red plastic lamp shaped like a mushroom, recent copies of *L'Express, Le Nouvel Observateur, Le Monde, Playboy* (the American edition), *L'Écho des Savanes* and other publications; and the LP racks with their symphony music, opera and *west coast* jazz records that were worth four or five thousand francs'. Manchette, *Le Petit Bleu de la côte ouest* (Paris: Éditions Gallimard, 1976), 30. A translation of *Le Petit Bleu* has been published as *Three to Kill*, trans. Donald Nicolson-Smith (San Francisco: City Lights, 2002).

The corollary of this obsession with objects is an appreciable and uneasy sense of depersonalization. Georges's daughters remain through out 'les fillettes', nameless, and barely distinguishable from the haze of objects around him. Georges worries about staining his Mercedes car seats with the injured man's blood in ch. 3 rather than pondering his suffering. Indeed, in an astute piece of textual play, the description of the Mercedes interior and of Georges's inner world are interwined to exacerbate the pervasive and shocking sense of an equivalence between people and things: 'Georges est un homme de moins de quarante ans. Sa voiture est une Mercedes gris acier. Le cuir des sièges est acajou, et de même l'ensemble des décorations intérieures de l'automobile. L'intérieur de Georges Gerfaut est sombre et confus, on y distingue vaguement des idées de gauche.'[33]

This critique of consumer culture is heightened in the novel by the clinical use of a behaviourist style where all is described from the exterior. The reader is given no access to Georges's thoughts and denied any comforting identification with a *roman noir* hero on the run. The text is written in a characteristically minimalist prose style and presented from the viewpoint of a sardonic and detached narrator who looks down on Georges as the victim of a series of farcical incidents. Whilst Georges eventually guns down the hired killers, he remains a pathetic figure, at sea in events he does not understand. For Georges's adventures are a sign of the times. His is not an individual tale but representative of a generation: 'Georges est de son temps et aussi de son espace.'[34]

The space and time Georges inhabits share many features with a *néo-polar* vision of contemporary France. Although Georges himself experiences fleeting moments of existential crisis, these are far outweighed by his implication in interconnecting circles of violence. These begin in the home with bickers and squabbles between himself and Béa and ripple out into the workplace. Industrial disputes invade the offices and corridors at the headquarters of Georges's company ITT but barely register on Georges's conscious mind. The role of the mass media in masking such latent social violence is reinforced on several occasions as the reader is treated, in highly ironic mode, to Georges's perspective on the national and international news in the papers:

Gerfaut l'envoya [his secretary] en bas chercher *France-Soir* [. . .] Il fallait jouer le trois, le sept et le douze. Les chars et l'aviation étaient intervenus contre six

---

[33] 'Georges is a man under 40. His car is a steel-grey Mercedes. The leather upholstery is mahogany-brown as are the interior furnishings of the car. Georges's interior is sombre and muddled, vaguely left-wing ideas can be made out.' Manchette, *Le Petit Bleu*, 8.

[34] 'Georges is of his time and also of his place.' Manchette, *Le Petit Bleu*, 184.

mille paysans boliviens insurgés. Un Esquimau avait été abattu comme il
tentait de détourner un Boeing 747 sur la Corée du Nord. Un chalutier breton
avait disparu avec onze hommes à bord. Une centenaire venait d'avoir cent
ans et proclamait son intention de voter à gauche. Le gouvernement préparait
un train de mesures brutales. Des extraterrestres avaient volé un chien sous les
yeux de son propriétaire, un garde-barrière, dans le Bas-Rhin.³⁵

The ordering of news features shows up Manchette's cynical view of
reader interests and priorities; the lottery numbers first. Events of international proportions, civil war in Bolivia, are reduced to the same discursive level as the story of a German border guard who claims aliens stole his
dog. While tucked in between the bizarre human interest stories is the real
news of the day that all the others serve to occlude: the government is
planning a domestic crackdown. The presentation of the news here serves
to illustrate how individuals in this consumer culture are swamped by
competing narratives, unable to distinguish the ephemeral and banal
from events of social and political importance. State-sponsored violence
and repression is just another news item. However, this notion of latent
violence erupting into the everyday is brought to the fore for Georges by
the attempts on his life.

The killers, Carlo and Bastien, are a humorous parody of the contract
killer and his code of honour. Carlo's pledge to avenge his partner's death
after the fiasco at the petrol station is deliberately undercut by his reading
of a Spiderman comic over his partner's grave in deference to Bastien's
love for the comic-strip hero; God has been replaced by the power of popular culture to capture the imagination. Yet Manchette also makes it clear
that the contract killers form as integral a part of the capitalist economy
as the middle manager Georges. As David Platten notes, in Manchette's
world, 'the professional killer is the ultimate arbiter of market forces'.³⁶
Carlo and Bastien are not marginalized outsiders and their life as contract
killers is described as a career choice like any other, for industrialized
killing penetrates every sector of the economy: 'un cadre commercial,
pourtant, c'est normalement très facile à tuer. Carlo et Bastien pouvaient
faire des comparisons, car ils avaient exercé leur industrie dans les

³⁵ 'Gerfaut sent her [his secretary] downstairs to get *France-Soir*[...] You had to play the three, the
seven and the twelve. Tanks and aircraft had intervened to counter the insurrection of six thousand
Bolivian peasants. An Eskimo had been killed as he tried to divert a Boeing 747 to North Korea. A
Breton fishing trawler had disappeared with eleven men aboard. A 100-year old woman had just
celebrated her hundredth birthday and proclaimed her intention to vote for the Left. The government was drawing up draconian measures. Extra-terrestrials had stolen a dog right from under the
nose of its owner, a border guard in the Bas-Rhin.' Manchette, *Le Petit Bleu*, 39–40.
³⁶ David Platten, 'Reading Glasses, Guns and Robots: A History of Science in French Crime Fiction',
French Cultural Studies, 12/3 (October 2001), 253–70 (264).

couches les plus variées de la société.'[37] As the common element linking the stories of the Dominican exile and assassin, Emerich y Emerich, and the unexceptional marketing executive, Georges Gerfaut, they illustrate how it is not only money but violence that makes the wheels of the capitalist machine turn more effectively.

The role of the State as the prime motor for social violence and oppression colours the fictional universe of *Le Petit Bleu*. In the circles of violence that surround and invade Georges's life, Manchette reserves his most virulent attacks for state forces of law and order. Within a French context, Manchette makes reference to the repression of the Algerian war, identifying Georges's friend and ex-militant activist, Liétard, as a survivor of police brutality at the Charonne metro station.[38] His brutal attack on a lone policeman one night after his release from hospital is an enraged reaction to the trauma he has suffered at the hands of the police. At no point does Georges turn to the police for help or protection as Manchette effectively evacuates them from the narrative as representatives of order or justice. However, Manchette's targets go beyond the national frame and take on international dimensions with the character of Emerich y Emerich.

Chapter 2 of *Le Petit Bleu* breaks one of the formal rules of crime fiction; that is to build and maintain narrative momentum. At the end of ch. 1, the reader is confronted with the startling revelation that mild-mannered Georges has killed at least two men. Yet there then comes a long narrative digression as ch. 2 outlines the life of Emerich y Emerich. The purely descriptive nature of the chapter and the focus on past events in the Dominican Republic at first appear obscure to the reader. However, Emerich y Emerich, former head of secret services for the Dominican government, is the catalyst for the action of the novel. His life as a high-ranking functionary for a corrupt regime highlights the nexus of international forces that bear down on Georges's life, and that of other ordinary citizens of his generation, but which fail to register on their consciousness.

The representation of the Dominican Republic in ch. 2 exposes the links between the State, American corporate culture, the CIA, and the criminal underworld. Manchette's choice of Emerich y Emerich as the focalizer for this chapter makes it clear how intermingled these forces are and how they trigger violence and civil war. Emerich y Emerich exacts brutal torture, reminiscent of the atrocities of the Algerian war, on so-called 'class

---

[37] 'a commercial executive, however, is normally very easy to kill. Carlo and Bastien could make comparisons because they had practiced their trade on a wide cross-section of society.' Manchette, *Le Petit Bleu*, 76.

[38] On 8 February 1962, nine demonstrators died after police herded them into the blocked metro entrance as they demonstrated for Algerian independence.

enemies' as he benefits from the backing of Austin Motors and the CIA who rig supposedly free elections to install their preferred candidate. His smuggling and traffic in contraband goods is tolerated as the price of his loyalty as he crushes any embryonic democratic revolution that threatens to disrupt the smooth running of American business interests. As the workers rebel, they make Molotov cocktails out of the Pepsi-Cola bottles from the nearby factory in a neat image of the textual subversion Manchette himself enacts with his Marxist analysis of capitalism in the pages of a *polar*.

With the bloody killing of Emerich y Emerich and his bullmastiff Elisabeth in the last chapters of the text, it would seem that Georges has finally penetrated the obscure forces that have directed his life. *Le Petit Bleu* moves into more conventional *roman noir* mode as Georges turns detective and tracks down the dictator, turning from the hunted into the hunter. He would seem to have taken control of his life and made the connections between international capitalism, criminality, and social oppression that have disrupted his existence. But if the reader expects a moment of revelation on Georges's part, they are sadly disappointed. The novel ends with exactly the same image as it began: Georges circling on the Parisian *périphérique* under the influence of drink and drugs. All that seems to have changed is Georges's preference for 4 Roses bourbon rather than Cutty Sark Whisky.

On his return to his amazed wife after six months on the run, Georges claims amnesia and refuses to give any account of his previous adventures. His individual amnesia represents the collective refusal to see what the past and present indicate about the abuses of capitalism. Despite his temporary status as a perpetrator of violence in his bid for survival, Georges remains a victim of the system. Reversing a short paragraph that concludes the first chapter, Manchette ends the novel with an explanation for Georges's failure to free himself from the rat race:

> **Dans l'ensemble, ils vont être détruits, les rapports de production dans lesquels il faut chercher la raison pour laquelle Georges file ainsi sur la périphérique avec des réflexes diminués en écoutant cette musique-là. Peut-être Georges manifestera-t-il alors autre chose que la patience et la servilité qu'il a toujours manifestées. Ce n'est pas probable.**[39]

Individual rebellion can never overturn the social order; Georges can never occupy the place of the *roman noir* hero, able to retain some

---

[39] 'By and large, the relations of production will be destroyed which explain why George is driving along the ring road with diminished reflexes listening to this music. Then perhaps Georges will show something other than the patience and the servility that he has always shown. It is not likely.' Manchette, *Le Petit Bleu*, 183.

integrity in the face of social and political breakdown. Even in extreme circumstances, he cannot perceive the social 'lie' on which his life is based. Only the revolution to come can demolish the economic and political order on which his subjugation relies. The 'société de spectacle' reigns until collective actions can force change. Georges Gerfaut, unlike his namesake (*gerfaut* in French means a type of falcon), cannot fly away but is doomed to 'tourner en rond' (go round in circles).

Recuperation and renewal

Le Petit Bleu culminates in a poignant image of a man unable to escape from the conformity of his bourgeois existence in spite of having lived through extraordinary adventures. Georges Gerfaut's life epitomizes the dilemma that Manchette saw as dogging any attempt to resist the dominant economic and social order: recuperation. Not only would violent actions confirm the repressive state mechanisms in place (force must be met with force) but they risked being recouped by the dominant order to serve its own interests and perpetuate its system of power. This analysis of Georges's situation was to be repeated in Manchette's attitude towards his work as a *roman noir* writer. After having spoken eloquently of his aim to subvert the dominant capitalist order from within, he saw that his work had been recouped by the mass media. In a twist of fate, the writer who had so railed against the establishment was assimilated into the *roman noir* world and gave intellectual kudos to its production.

The recuperation of Manchette's work by conservative forces is best demonstrated by a number of film adaptations. As Manchette himself admitted, his books presented images of cinematographic precision that appealed to film directors. Yet, they were in fact very difficult to translate to the screen, not least because of the underlying themes and references that framed the scenes of violent action. It was, therefore, little surprise that the film adaptations of his later books were a travesty of his political and social critique, *Le Petit Bleu* perhaps more so than any other. Produced, adapted, and starring Alain Delon (a long time Gaullist), it was renamed *Trois hommes à abattre* (1980) and became a star vehicle for Delon himself. Directed by Jacques Deray, the film lifted the crime fiction intrigue of the novel (a man pursued by contract killers) but jettisoned Manchette's militant left-wing critique of capitalism. In the film, Gerfaut is no longer a loser and victim, but a professional gambler and playboy, the perfect parasite living off the money and glamour of consumer society. Played by Delon, it was inevitable that the film would conform to the formula of the action movie with car chases, explosions, and bloody killings. Gerfaut turns the tables on his pursuers in the film and is consistently mistaken for a professional hit man, in keeping with Delon's screen persona as the cool and distant killer in such films as Jean-Pierre Melville's *Les Samouraï* (1967). A political dimension is retained as the killing upon which Gerfaut stumbles is part of a plot to cover up secrets in the French arms industry. This does not, however, implicate the wider economic or social order and Gerfaut's death at the end is presented as the order protecting itself from outside threats.

Manchette seems to have accepted the butchery of his novel sanguinely, remarking that a text is not a sacred object and that a book and its film adaptation are two separate creative endeavours. Yet the creative distance that he took with regard to film adaptations could not disguise his disappointment as a novelist who had been so influenced by cinema (he claimed that the exploding petrol station scene in *Le Petit Bleu* was inspired by Hitchcock's *North by Northwest*). The prospective of further recuperation by the critical establishment may explain why Manchette published no further *romans noirs* in the last fifteen years of his life. He too may have suffered from a fear that he had nothing new to say, the leitmotif of repetition and turning in circles in *Le Petit Bleu* being a premonition of this. In 1981, he published his last novel, *La Position du tireur couché* and there followed fifteen years of 'silence' when he continued to meditate on the form and possibilities of the *roman noir* through his crime fiction columns and translations. An unfinished novel, *La Princesse de sang*, was published posthumously in 1996 and indicated the extent to which the last years of his life had been consumed in the elaboration of new directions for the *roman noir*. The narrative showed how he had attempted to combine the spy thriller, the *roman noir*, and elements of fantasy for a geo-political critique of the contemporary era.

Manchette's novels and critical writing represent a sophisticated critique of the capitalist culture of his day. If Baudrillard, Perec, and others were prepared to analyse the social, psychological, and economic effects of consumerism, Manchette went one step further in couching his attack on such values in a radical political vision. The violence of contemporary society and its materialist dreams is set forth in an insurrectionary prose that aims at the overthrow of the capitalist order itself. However, by the early 1980s, such a revolutionary venture seemed outmoded. The collective uprising and social transformation writers such as Manchette hoped would succeed May 1968 failed to materialize and the victory of the Left in parliamentary elections in 1981 was largely a disappointment. Unlike his character Georges Gerfaut, by the mid-1980s Manchette was no longer of his time or his place.

This too seemed to be case for the *néo-polar*. For if Manchette remained a reference point for younger writers, his theoretically informed writing was superseded by a new form of *roman noir engagé* (the committed *roman noir*). Left-leaning detective fiction writers of the 1980s were less concerned with revolution than investigating specific social and political issues in France, such as nuclear power and environmental pollution, immigration and social deprivation, crimes of state and recent French history. Politically active in a number of cases, writers like Didier Daeninckx and Thierry Jonquet came to the *roman noir* with an ethical agenda that sought to denounce abuses of power and raise awareness in their readers. The emblematic figure for this morally charged renewal of the *roman noir* was the renegade policeman, the representative of law and order who challenged the system from within. In the case of Didier Daeninckx, his Inspector Cadin was to act as the conscience of the nation in his investigation of state crimes against humanity.

4 Historical Investigations: Didier Daeninckx, *Meurtres pour mémoire* (1984)

Le roman noir est le récit d'une guerre privée entre la vérité et le mensonge, entre la fiction et le réel: le réel ment. La fiction reste le seul moyen de le subvertir et de le faire avouer.[1]

Memories of conflict, conflicting memories

In France, the 1980s were characterized by a resurgence of interest in the Second World War. Many factors contributed to this phenomenon. Prominent amongst these were the elaboration of new historical models for examining the recent past, particularly studies of individual and collective memories, the high profile of public debates and commemorations to mark the fortieth anniversary of key wartime events, and the sense of a generation passing away who had directly experienced the Occupation. For the Second World War represents a troubling period in French history, one where personal and collective memories do not always coincide with official versions in the public domain. There has rarely been consensus over the history and legacy of the Second World War and, over the post-war era, alternative accounts have made their impact felt on an evolving national discourse. Over the decades, writers, film-makers, and historians have all played their part in challenging dominant representations of the Occupation and the power they confer on social and political élites.[2] However, the 1980s signalled a high point in the re-visioning of such years. For historian Henry Rousso, they heralded a period of 'obsession' and were the latest manifestation of what he labelled the 'Vichy syndrome'.[3]

For Rousso, the key feature of this obsessive return to the Occupation in 1980s France was the focus on Jewish memories of persecution and

---

[1] 'The *roman noir* is the story of a private war between truth and lies, between fiction and reality: reality lies. Fiction remains the only means of undermining it and forcing a confession.' Maurice G. Dantec quoted in Jean Pons, 'Le Roman noir, littérature réelle', *Les Temps modernes*, 595 (August–October 1997), 11.

[2] See Alan Morris, *Collaboration and Resistance Reviewed: Writers and the Mode Retro in Post-Gaullist France* (Oxford: Berg, 1992).

[3] See Henry Rousso, *Le Syndrome de Vichy: de 1944 à nos jours*, 2nd edn. (Paris: Seuil, 1990).

deportation. During the war years, the collaborating Vichy government contributed to some of the worst crimes against humanity committed on French soil by lending its assistance to the Nazi 'Final Solution'. In France, over 75,000 Jewish men, women, and children were rounded up and deported to extermination camps in the east. Only 2,500 returned. Although the genocide was conceived and set in place by the Nazis, French policemen, civil servants, and military units facilitated the work of the German invaders by rounding up and detaining Jews. Convoys were sent from all over France to transit centres, like Drancy in the suburbs of Paris, before deportation to death camps, such as Auschwitz-Birkenau.

The extent of French state collaboration in the mechanisms of the Holocaust was the subject of grounding-breaking work in the 1980s. American historians Michael Marrus and Robert Paxton highlighted how the Vichy regime had anticipated German orders and set in place its own anti-Semitic legislation aimed at the exclusion of French Jews from the national community.[4] Throughout the decade, a substantial number of books appeared on Vichy and the Jews, as well as on the regime's persecution of other groups, such as gypsies, Communists, and foreign exiles. French Jewish lawyer and historian Serge Klarsfeld campaigned for recognition of the victims of such policies and demanded that those responsible be brought to justice. By the end of the decade, the Vichy regime could no longer be regarded as an aberration in French history but rather as the product of a long line of right-wing, anti-democratic traditions.[5]

These historical reinterpretations of the Occupation were complemented by a wave of Holocaust testimonies. Towards the end of their lives, many French survivors published memoirs of their experiences in the concentration camps. In what Annette Wieviorka has called the 'era of the witness',[6] the imperative to remember became a rallying cry for those who wished the French State to acknowledge its complicity in the persecution and extermination of Jews in France. Children of persecuted Jews wrote their family histories, showing how memories of the wartime past had been transmitted from one generation to another, often with deeply troubling consequences. Yet, these memories of the Occupation had also to be put alongside the accounts of children of collaborators and resisters. Their narratives too illustrated the ongoing tensions and contradictions that made up intersecting group memories of the Occupation.

---

[4] Michael Marrus and Robert Paxton, *Vichy France and the Jews* (New York: Basic Books, 1981).
[5] For an overview of historiographical trends in studies of the Occupation, see Julian Jackson, 'Introduction: Historians and the Occupation', *France: The Dark Years 1940–1944* (Oxford: Oxford University Press, 2001), 1–20.   [6] See Annette Wieviorka, *L'Ère du témoin* (Paris: Plon, 1998),

One of the flashpoints to illustrate the conflicts surrounding the history and memory of the Occupation were the first attempts to indict former Vichy civil servants and officials for crimes against humanity in the early 1980s. A parliamentary vote in 1964 ended the statute of limitations on crimes against humanity, enabling the French courts to pursue war criminals long after the events in question had passed. Such legislation was aimed primarily at Germans who had operated in France during the war years, such as Klaus Barbie, the 'butcher of Lyon', a former Gestapo chief who was extradited from Bolivia in 1983 and eventually tried and sentenced to life imprisonment in 1987. However, from the late 1970s onwards, this legislation was turned on French perpetrators of war crimes, specifically those involved in the deportation of Jews. Jean Leguay, René Bousquet, Paul Touvier, and Maurice Papon were all the subject of juridical investigations, with Touvier and Papon eventually brought before the French courts in the 1990s.[7] Whilst Leguay and Bousquet had been tried at the Liberation as collaborators, others, such as Papon, had not and none had been tried for their role in the Final Solution. The trials of the 1990s offered, therefore, the tantalizing possibility of holding the Vichy regime to account.

The case of Maurice Papon in particular was to rock the foundations of post-war French Republicanism. For he was implicated not only in crimes committed under the Vichy regime but also during the troubled post-war history of French decolonization, particularly the Algerian war. Secretary-general of the Gironde prefecture from 1942 to 1944, Papon had begun a brilliant administrative career under the pre-war Third Republic and continued in his post after the Occupation. Responsible for 'Jewish affairs' in the Bordeaux region, Papon was in charge of the deportation of over 1,500 Jews from the area to Drancy, enacting anti-Semitic directives that emanated from his superiors in Vichy. Yet he deftly created a Resistance record for himself prior to the defeat of Germany and its allies and de Gaulle appointed him prefect of the Gironde immediately after the Liberation.

Under the Fourth and Fifth Republics, Papon remained a stalwart of successive French administrations and was nominated to important colonial posts during the late 1940s and 1950s. These included a stint as inspector-general of North-Eastern Algeria from 1956 to 1958 at the height of the Algerian war. Under Papon's leadership, torture and the massive transfer of populations were used as key weapons in the war against nationalist sympathizers and activists. In 1958, he supported the

[7] Jean Leguay was indicted in March 1979, Paul Touvier in 1981, Maurice Papon in 1983 (and again, after the case was quashed, in 1988), and René Bousquet in 1991.

second rise to power of Charles de Gaulle with the founding of the Fifth
Republic and served a term as Paris Chief of Police from 1958 to 1967.
During this period, he oversaw the brutal police repression of a peaceful
demonstration in favour of Algerian independence on 17 October 1961.
The official death toll of three dead and some sixty wounded was later to
be challenged, with some historians estimating the number at between
two and three hundred killed. In the 1970s, Papon served as a budget
minister in a Conservative administration but his glittering career ended
in 1981 when his wartime past was exposed in an issue of the satirical
magazine, *Le Canard enchaîné*.

As a career civil servant, Papon's professional itinerary straddled the
civil service, foreign affairs, and the French economy. He had worked with
and for many of the major institutions of the modern French State and he
had been connected with some of the most venerated French political
figures of the day. His trial for crimes against humanity raised the spectre
of investigating not only France's wartime past but also state crimes from
other periods of French history—from wartime anti-Semitism to the
'dirty' history of decolonization. His pervasive presence in French political life meant that, for American historian Richard Golsan, 'in reality,
the trial was less an exercise whose purpose was to come to terms with
the past than the expression of a complete loss of faith in the nation-state
as the guarantor of the rights of the individual'.[8]

As Charles Forsdick has argued, investigating memories of the recent
past in France can be envisaged as an exercise in 'déminage' (mine clear-
ance).[9] Excavating one layer of memory may well uncover memories of
another conflict that, like a time bomb, risk disturbing long-held values
and assumptions about contemporary French identity. Maurice Papon is
a case in point and the convoluted process to bring him to justice illustrated how far members of the French political establishment were prepared to go to avoid confronting the ethical dilemmas raised by his career.
However, one privileged arena in which such issues were discussed during the 1980s and 1990s was fiction, and more particularly crime fiction.
As a genre, the crime novel calls on the reader to delve into the past in
order to solve the crime at hand. It is in essence a narrative in search
of a 'lost' story of murder and death and works to elucidate questions of
individual and collective guilt. By focusing that quest on the recent past, a
group of French *roman noir* writers in the 1980s contested the selective

---

[8] 'Introduction', in Richard J. Golsan (ed.), *Memory and Justice on Trial: The Papon Affair* (London: Routledge, 2000), 29.

[9] Charles Forsdick, ' "Direction les oubliettes de l'histoire": Witnessing the Past in the Contemporary French Polar', *French Cultural Studies*, 12/3 (October 2002), 333–50 (338).

silences of the French State and proposed new readings of events that
have profoundly marked French national identity.

The French *roman noir engagé* of the 1980s

French crime fiction entered the literary mainstream during the 1980s.
This was a period when some prominent *roman noir* writers crossed the
divide between *littérature noire* (crime fiction) and *littérature blanche*
(mainstream fiction). Jean Vautrin, Daniel Pennac, and Pierre Magnan all
won critical recognition for their work and were subsequently published
in prestigious mainstream collections. Much of the impetus for the
changing status of the *roman noir* can be attributed to the socio-political
context of the 1980s. The *néo-polar* had paved the way for the *roman noir*
to be considered as a significant cultural phenomenon, appealing to an
intellectually discerning and politically active audience in the aftermath
of May 1968. The 1970s offered the hope of social revolution but, with
the election of a Socialist government in 1981, many of those on the Left
who had expected great things were disappointed. Their response was to
withdraw from the political mainstream. Yet, one of the few literary forms
in which a *gauchiste* vision of French life persisted was the *roman noir*. A
large number of celebrated French authors writing during the 1980s were
former left-wing militants who came to the *roman noir* as a genre of
protest writing. This is not to claim a left-wing sensibility for all *roman
noir* writing of the decade but the form certainly became a key vehicle for
disaffected French radicals who used it to find a political voice.[10]

In the 1980s, a generation of detective fiction writers moved to ground
the *roman noir* in contemporary reality. Authors, such as Didier Daeninckx
and Thierry Jonquet, produced texts that are as much a social history of
their times as a murder intrigue. The setting and topics around which
their books were structured were painstakingly researched: from physical
and mental abuse in care homes and the politics of the nuclear power
industry to life as a homeless person on the Parisian metro.[11] Such writ-
ings are infused with a crusading spirit that rejects the ironic detachment
and parodic tone of much *néo-polar* writing. In the hands of such writers,

[10] See the dossier 'Le Polar: entre critique sociale et désenchantement', in *Mouvements*, 15/16
(May–August 2001), 5–7, for an astute assessment of the development of the French and Italian
roman noir in the 1970s and 1980s.
[11] These themes are addressed respectively in Jonquet, *Mémoire en cage* (1982) and Daeninckx, *Mort
au premier tour* (1982) and *Métropolice* (1985).

the *roman noir* is aimed at educating the reader and sensibilizing them to French socio-economic problems.

In a special issue of *Les Temps modernes* devoted to the *roman noir*, its editor Jean Pons describes this contemporary French crime novel as a *roman noir engagé*—committed crime writing. For Pons, the *roman noir* is a form of writing whose heroes serve to diagnose the social ills of their age and whose mission is to 'approfondir le sens des choses, de les mettre en relations, de trouver une profondeur cachée'.[12] Like an investigative journalist, the *roman noir* writer seeks to uncover the 'insider story' of social exclusion and deprivation and to expose the activities of powerful economic and political interest groups. As Pons repeatedly emphasizes, the *roman noir* is far from being a *roman 'policier'* in the service of the State. It reveals instead the failure of the forces of law and order to maintain social cohesion and the lies and obfuscations that enable the ruling classes to retain power. One of the major campaigns around which the left-wing credentials of the *roman noir* crystallized during the 1980s was opposition to Far Right political parties and associations. Their public profile had increased significantly with the electoral success of the Front National in local, national, and European elections. *Roman noir* writers, such as Daeninckx, took on the racist and xenophobic pronouncements of the party in a battle of words that contested their views and ideology.

Writing a *roman noir engagé* in the 1980s was perceived, therefore, as part of a broader strategy of political intervention. As Annie Collovold has argued, for committed writers, adopting the genre meant that 'une politique d'intervention littéraire s'est peu à peu substituée à l'intervention politique en littérature'.[13] Individual writers were ready and willing to adopt a public persona that made them spokespeople for communities afflicted by racism, social violence, and poverty. They used their literary success as a platform for denouncing government policies or campaigning for issues that were of particular concern to them as informed French citizens. According to writer Gérard Delteil, this did not always make them popular with established political parties and associations, even those on the radical Left with whom they had a natural affinity.[14] Speaking out with passion at the state of local government or foreign affairs, individual *roman noir* writers carved out a role as maverick figures. They appeared as populist intellectuals who refused to endorse a

[12] 'to deepen an understanding of things, to relate them to one another, to find hidden depths'. Pons, 'Le roman noir, littérature réelle', 5–14 (8).

[13] 'a politics of literary intervention was replaced little by little by political interventions in literature'. Annie Collovald, 'L'Enchantement dans la désillusion politique', *Mouvements*, 15/16, 16–21 (21).

[14] Gérard Delteil, 'La vie est un roman noir et nous y sommes tous engagés', *Les Temps modernes*, 595, 172–80 (179).

predetermined ideological agenda and expressed their moral outrage in highly polemical terms.

The French crime writers who took up the mantle of literary commitment in the 1980s reinvented the *roman noir* for their times. Daeninckx, Frédéric Fajardie, Jean-François Vilar, Thierry Jonquet, and Jean-Bernard Pouy all chose to retain their grassroots *gauchiste* affiliations and to adopt the *roman noir* as a vehicle for a wide-ranging social and political critique. Their contribution to the genre is such that today the early 1980s are considered a turning point in the French tradition and as an era during which the French *roman noir* developed a specific voice. Ultimately, the 1980s liberated the French *roman noir* from the ghetto of *paralittérature*, or formula fiction, and set it on a course that would intersect with developments in the literary mainstream.

Didier Daeninckx and the thriller of historical memory

Didier Daeninckx is the leading figure amongst this group of committed *roman noir* writers. Born into a working-class family in Aubervilliers in the suburbs of Paris, Daeninckx's choice of the *roman noir* is coloured by a family history of left-wing activism. Many of the relatives and friends whom Daeninckx describes in numerous interviews were implicated in traumatic events in French national history. His paternal grandfather deserted during the First World War and narrowly avoided the firing squad. His maternal grandfather was elected as one of the youngest Communist mayors in France in 1935 but was expelled from the party after he expressed opposition to the Germano-Soviet pact during the Second World War. During the 1950s and 1960s, Daeninckx's mother militated for the independence of France's colonies, while a close family friend, Suzanne Martorell, was one of eight victims crushed to death when police herded peaceful demonstrators into the closed entrance of the Charonne metro station in February 1962.[15]

Daeninckx's novels work through this troubled family history, crisscrossed by the major crises of the twentieth century. Fictional families are torn apart and decimated by war and national upheaval, while the crimes of one generation are revisited upon the next. In two novels, *Meurtres pour mémoire* (1984) and *La Mort n'oublie personne* (1989), sons pay with

---

[15] Daeninckx talks of the demonstration and its brutal police repression as the foundational moment for his *roman noir* career. See 'Entretien avec Didier Daeninckx: une modernité contre la modernité de pacotilles', in *Mouvements*, 15/16, 9–15.

their lives when the past of their fathers comes to haunt the present. At one level, this focus on a familial heritage can be interpreted as Daeninckx exorcizing demons from his own life history. Yet, on a more general level, translating national events and tragedies into such personalized encounters is also a pointed reminder that recent history can never be divorced from its impact on individuals.

Daeninckx began writing *romans noirs* in the late 1970s and published his first novel, *La Mort au premier tour*, in 1982 in the classic mystery collection Le Masque. This breakthrough into the publishing world brought him to the attention of the Série noire and, between 1984 and 1986, he produced six novels for the series before moving on to publish in more mainstream literary collections.[16] In terms of Daeninckx's profile as an *écrivain engagé* (committed writer), he has positioned himself as an outspoken opponent of racism and right-wing extremism. In recent years, he has championed causes such as the plight of immigrants without residency papers and opposed the rise of the Front National and the media profile of French Holocaust deniers. Indeed, his attacks on 'rouges-bruns', or left-wing intellectuals who contest the existence or extent of the Holocaust, have led to heated exchanges in the press.[17] Such a campaigning role has prompted some writers and critics to accuse him of pursuing an overly didactic and moralizing agenda: 'Daeninckx se voit en redresseur de torts, en rédempteur. Il croit qu'il a une mission à accomplir.'[18] For others, this is less a personal crusade than a genuine attempt to expose the subterfuges and silences of the ruling classes over deep-rooted anti-democratic traditions in French public life.

As a *roman noir* writer, Daeninckx's novels inevitably reflect his personal and political concerns. The main focus of his work is on memory and more particularly the ways in which traces of the past resurface to trouble the present: 'car le passé n'est jamais mort: il constitue une dimension essentielle, irréductible, du présent'.[19] This has led critics Claude Prévost and Jean-Claude Lebrun to categorize his novels as 'le thriller de la mémoire historique'.[20] With the precision of a professional historian, Daeninckx investigates troubling episodes in French history: from the carnage of the First World War to the infamous 1986 exclusion

---

[16] Daeninckx has recently returned to the Série noire with *12, rue Meckert* (2001).

[17] One figure whom Daeninckx has denounced for such views is the writer and journalist Gilles Perrault in *Le Goût de la vérité* (Paris: Éditions Verdier, 1997).

[18] 'Daeninckx believes himself to be a righter of wrongs, a redeemer. He thinks he has a mission to fulfil.' Luc Le Vaillant, 'Le Rouge-noir', *Libération*, 14 March 1997.

[19] 'because the past is always with us: it constitutes an essential, irreducible dimension of the present'. Daeninckx, *Le Goût de la vérité*, 152.

[20] 'the thriller of historical memory'. Claude Prévost and Jean-Claude Lebrun, 'Profil Didier Daeninckx', in *Nouveaux territoires romanesques* (Paris: Messidor, 1990), 83.

laws of the then Minister of the Interior, Charles Pasqua.[21] With detailed knowledge of archival material as well a concern to show the intersection of place and personal history, Daeninckx's novels are renown for their attention to the texture of history. Yet this memory work is never a neutral activity for Daeninckx devotes it to exposing the partial histories that serve those in power.

In Daeninckx's fictional universe, characters work to elucidate the truth behind the official version of events. In *Meurtres pour mémoire,* as in other early novels featuring Inspector Cadin, his mission is to question the ways in which history has been transmitted. Cadin constantly comes up against the stubborn resistance of those in power to confront shameful aspects of twentieth-century French history. For reasons of political expediency and self-interest, the official state institutions prefer to suppress bloody episodes in recent memory. What remains therefore is an incomplete history, one that is told from only one point of view. Dissonant voices and accounts are erased and, in their place, a fiction is erected that glosses over inconsistencies and ambiguities. In Daeninckx's novels, it is the work of the detective-historian to expose such fictions as a lie. This is a process that involves recuperating stories of the past and uncovering how and why alternative histories have been lost to the public record. As writing against the establishment, such texts serve to destabilize the monolithic narratives of the State and to hint at a parallel but largely marginalized history of repression.

Meurtres pour mémoire: 'un passé qui ne passe pas'[22]

Daeninckx's second novel, *Meurtres pour mémoire* (1984), created a media sensation when it was published in the Série noire. It received the Prix Paul Vaillant-Couturier in 1984 and the Grand Prix de la Littérature Policière in 1985, so consecrating Daeninckx as the leading light of his generation of *roman noir* writers. The novel tells the story of father and son historians, Roger and Bernard Thiraud, one murdered during the brutal police suppression of a demonstration on the 17 October 1961, the other gunned down in Toulouse over twenty years later in similarly mysterious circumstances. Inspector Cadin is put in charge of the investigation

---

[21] See respectively, *Le Der des ders* (1985) and *Lumière noire* (1987).

[22] Taken from the title of Eric Conan and Henry Rousso's *Vichy, un passé qui ne passe pas* (Paris: Fayard, 1994). As Nathalie Morello kindly pointed out, this phrase has a double meaning: a past that will not pass away, as well as a past that cannot be digested or stomached.

into Bernard's death and, like a historian, follows a paper trail of clues that connect Bernard's murder to that of his father, Roger. The missing link is the history of Drancy, the Jewish transit centre in wartime Paris that is the subject of an incomplete monograph study by Thiraud senior and taken up by his son many years later. For it emerges that the same official, André Veillut, presided over the transport of Jews from the Toulouse region to Drancy during the war years as directed the bloody massacre of North African demonstrators in 1961. In a bid to suppress his dark wartime past, the civil servant in question orchestrates the murder of Roger Thiraud, an innocent bystander to the 1961 demonstration, and later kills Bernard himself in the streets of Toulouse. Veillut is finally tracked down and murdered by the ageing secret agent who assassinated Roger Thiraud, tricked into believing the historian to be a political subversive. A form of retributive justice concludes the novel but there is no resolution over if and how France as a nation has come to terms with its past.

As this plot summary makes clear, Daeninckx's novel is a scarcely veiled reworking of the Papon case in fictional format. Daeninckx would later describe the book as 'un véritable manifeste littéraire, politique et moral',[23] setting out the key themes and values that would inform his later writing. Yet as Charles Forsdick points out in his insightful analysis, the novel is also a carefully calculated intervention in the debates of the day: 'a historical document in two senses, as a result not only of its subject matter, but also of its active role—alongside the subsequent series of historical accounts—in restoring memories of the recent French past'.[24] For Daeninckx chooses to appropriate the *roman noir* format for a history of the recent past that challenges reader expectations. He defamiliarizes history, providing a 'history from below' that focuses on the victims of French state aggression. As a historical investigation, *Meurtres pour mémoire* asks readers to search their own consciences as French citizens and to judge those who set themselves up as the political and moral arbiters of the nation.

Meurtres pour mémoire begins with the intersecting stories of three individuals: Saïd Milache, Roger Thiraud, and Kaïra Guelanine. In the first two chapters of the book, they are the main figures in what Josiane Peltier has described as 'a sort of Marxist detective novel in which the oppressed are repositioned as the central agents, even if they are the physical victims, of a particular historical moment'.[25] Such a literary strategy underscores

---

[23] 'a veritable literary, political and moral manifesto'. Didier Daeninckx, *Écrire en contre: Entretiens avec Robert Deleuse, Christine Cadet, Philippe Videlier* (Vénissieux: Éditions Paroles de l'Aube, 1997), 123.

[24] Forsdick, 'Witnessing the Past in the French Polar', 343.

[25] Josiane Peltier, 'Didier Daeninckx and Michel de Certeau: A Historiography of Affects', in Mullen and O'Beirne (eds.), *Crime Scenes: Detective Narratives in European Culture since 1945*, 269–80 (272).

Daeninckx's interest in a 'histoire vécue' (lived history) and the voices of those who have been effectively obliterated from official accounts. The sections devoted to Saïd and Kaïra are particularly evocative as Daeninckx reconstructs the lives of an Algerian immigrant community in 1960s Paris. Such micro-histories highlight the cultural hybridity and integration of this group; the young Aounit herds his father's sheep on nearby wasteland astride his moped but looks forward to the next football match against the team from rue de la République. The presentation of Kaïra shows how a young Algerian woman benefited from the relative emancipation of living in a less traditionally gendered society. Able to wear trousers and be seen with a companion, Kaïra attains a degree of freedom unheard of for previous generations of Algerian women.

All three life histories meet on the evening of 17 October 1961 at 7.25 p.m. near Bonne Nouvelle metro station as Roger, on his way home from watching the horror film *Le Récupérateur des cadavres*,[26] stumbles upon a demonstration of Algerians opposed to new draconian curfew conditions. These have been imposed on North Africans living and working in Paris and are justified by claims that they represent a terrorist threat in metropolitan France. As the three individual identities merge with the crowds around them, a detached omniscient narrator recounts the events of the night. The French riot police are presented as robotic, faceless killers who show no mercy or compassion. As the police photographer later recounts, 'mais des C.R.S. me demandaient de les prendre dans la pose du chasseur, le pied sur le corps d'un Algérien'[27]—a gruesome echo of the colonial struggle taking place overseas at this time. In contrast, the demonstrators are shown to be helpless victims, men, women, and children, unarmed and totally unaware of what awaits them on the main boulevards of Paris.

Daeninckx reserves his worst condemnation for the local Parisians who look on and refuse to intervene in what Cadin describes as 'un Oradour en plein Paris'.[28] The local theatre producer of the ironically named 'Adieu Prudence' refuses refuge to those demonstrators being pursued by the

---

[26] The references to popular culture and particularly film are highly significant in Daeninckx's fictional reconstruction of 17 October 1961. The screening of *Le Récupérateur de cadavres* (The Body Snatcher) is an intimation of Inspector Cadin's future investigation as he resurrects the life histories of the demonstrators to solve the crime.

[27] 'some of the French riot police asked me to photograph them like big game hunters—with their foot on the body of an Algerian'. Daeninckx, *Meurtres pour mémoire* (Paris: Gallimard, 1984), 92. An English-language version is published as *Murder in Memoriam*, trans. Liz Heron (London: Serpent's Tail, 1991).

[28] 'an Oradour in the middle of Paris', Daeninckx, *Meurtres pour mémoire*, 81. This is a loaded reference to the shooting and burning of over 600 villagers at Oradour sur Glâne by retreating German troops at the liberation of France during the Second World War.

police and worries that the confusion and chaos will delay his opening night. Another passer-by claims that the Algerian demonstrators deserve their treatment: 'Ils l'ont bien cherché . . . Si vous croyez qu'ils ont pitié des nôtres, là-bas. Et d'abord ce sont eux qui ont tiré les premiers.'[29] In this bloody scene of police violence set against the unspoken backdrop of the Algerian war, Roger Thiraud stands out as the only witness to register the violations of basic human rights. The reader shares his horrified view-point and incomprehension at the blatant racism and brutality of the police.

The novel's condemnation of the mistreatment of immigrants and others perceived as undesirables is a recurrent feature in Daeninckx's representation of urban life. As Kristin Ross notes, Daeninckx sets forth the co-ordinates of a 'deep history' of French racism and anti-Semitism that surfaces not only in the banal conversation of taxi drivers ('à inter-valles régulières, le chauffeur tentait de lancer la conversation sur les tares de conduite comparées des Arabes et des Africains')[30] but also in the topography of the city.[31] The third historian in the text, Bernard's girlfriend, Claudine Chenet, unearths this 'deep history' of intolerance and prejudice in her research into the communities who lived and worked on the site of the old fortifications of Paris after their demolition in 1920. Her work is an attempt to deconstruct how place has a defining impact on memories of the recent past.

Claudine visits what remains of this once thriving area, now a conven-tional Parisian suburb, and analyses how and why it gained a reputation as a hotbed of criminality. Her research leads her to focus on representa-tions of the poor and excluded over the twentieth century and to contest the stories of violence, murder, and theft that circulated about them to the benefit of the ruling classes. Investigating these physical vestiges of the past, Chenet shows up how successive generations of immigrants have been used as scapegoats for national fears and anxieties. Their demoniza-tion has enabled those in power to play on collective prejudices as a means of social control. The link to the present and the current preoccupation with 'insécurité' (law and order) is a worrying trend: 'Les brébis galeuses sont maintenant ceux qui logent dans les grands ensembles, en lointaines

---

29 'they were looking for trouble [. . .] if you think that they show any pity for our lads over there. And, anyway, it was them who started shooting first'. Daeninckx, *Meurtres pour mémoire*, 34.

30 'at regular intervals, the taxi driver attempted to start up a conversation on the relative defects of Arabs and Africans'. Daeninckx, *Meurtres pour mémoire*, 88.

31 See Kristin Ross's analysis of the detective as 'cognitive cartographer' in 'Watching the Detectives', in Frances Barker, Peter Hulme, and Margaret Inerson (eds.), *Postmodernism and the Re-reading of Modernity* (Manchester: Manchester University Press, 1992), 46–56.

banlieues . . . . Les immigrés ont remplacé les romanichels, les jeunes chômeurs ont pris la place des biffins.'[32]

If the representation of the forces of law and order is so uniformly negative in the early chapters of the book, the character of Inspector Cadin offers Daeninckx the chance to tell a more complex history of the recent past from the viewpoint of the lawmakers. As Daeninckx's first serial detective, Cadin operates at the intersection of history and justice.[33] He is the epitome of the 'flic contestataire', the renegade policeman who exposes the corruption of the system from within but at a high personal price. As Daeninckx has discussed in interview, Cadin was conceived as 'un pur produit des questionnements de l'après-soixante-huit',[34] ready and willing to challenge the status quo in the pursuit of social justice. Yet throughout his fictional life, Cadin remains out of step with his times and those around him and painfully aware of the injustices of contemporary society.[35] He is a character burdened with an acute social conscience that makes him an isolated figure in the police world, constantly moved on from one posting to the next and labelled as a troublemaker. In his final incarnation as an alcoholic private detective in the short story collection *Le Facteur fatal* (1990) the spiralling despair of his life ends with suicide at 11.59 p.m. on 31 December 1989. It would seem that with his *gauchiste* values and ideals, Cadin cannot survive into a post-Cold War world.

In *Meurtres pour mémoire*, the reader first encounters Cadin during a gravediggers' strike in Toulouse. This image of Cadin attempting to negotiate between the municipal authorities and the gravediggers who want a bonus for exhuming bodies from the last twenty years operates as a *mise en abyme* of the project of the book. The gravediggers object to their working conditions claiming that 'aujourd'hui on sort les macchabées des années soixante. L'âge d'or du plastique . . . Je ne vous fais pas de dessein mais les os, je vous jure, on ne les voit plus souvent!'[36] Just as the

---

[32] 'the black sheep are now those who live in the big council estates in far-off suburbs. Immigrants have replaced the gypsies, the young unemployed have taken the place of the rag pickers.' Daeninckx, *Meurtres pour mémoire*, 133–4.

[33] Cadin appeared as the main protagonist in four novels: *Mort au premier tour* (1982), *Meurtres pour mémoire* (1984), *Le Géant inachevé* (1984), *Le Bourreau et son double* (1986), and a short story collection, *Le Facteur fatal* (1990). He is a peripheral character in the novel *Lumière noire* (1987) and features in the short story 'Main courante' (1994).

[34] 'a pure product of post-'68 questioning'. Daeninckx, *Écrire en contre*, 13. Daeninckx relates Cadin to two other maverick police investigators created in the aftermath of May 1968: Manchette's ex-riot squad detective Eugène Tarpon and Jean Amila's hippy cop, Géronimo.

[35] See Jean-Pierre Deloux's fictional biography of Cadin, 'Grandeurs et servitudes policières . . .', *Polar*, 3 (1991), 9–24.

[36] 'today we dig up corpses from the 1960s. The golden age of plastic . . . I won't draw you a picture but I swear we don't see too many bones anymore'. Daeninckx, *Meurtres pour mémoire*, 45.

gravediggers baulk at the atrocious state of bodies from the 1960s so Cadin's role will be to resurrect the lives and identities of those from the 1961 demonstration in order to tell their story and see that a form of justice is done. This metaphorical exhumation will, however, involve going further back in time and revisiting another period, the war years, where even fewer traces remain of individual lives.

Cadin's dual investigation of the Occupation and the history of French decolonization takes on the appearance of a historical research project. Where other official bodies refuse to collate the material, Cadin's work takes him to secret police files, regional archives, and to interview key witnesses. Speaking to Mme Thiraud, Cadin is the first policeman to encourage her to tell the story of witnessing her husband's murder from her apartment window. Cadin also interviews the disgraced police photographer Marc Rosner and travels to Belgium to see uncut film footage of the 1961 demonstration, allowing him to identify Roger Thiraud's killer. Reading too the unfinished monograph by Roger and Bernard Thiraud on their hometown of Drancy, Cadin makes the final connections that link French crimes against humanity with the individual tragedies of the Thiraud family.

Cadin's breakthrough relies as much on an imaginative identification with the victims of state-sanctioned killing as on the processes of investigation and rational deduction. It is one of the innovations of Daeninckx's novel to foreground the ethical dimension of Cadin's quest for truth, for it is only when Cadin can visualize the victims and their plight that he is able to move towards some form of resolution. This is particularly the case for the Jewish children of Drancy. They first enter the narrative as statistical data, defined as units of milk whose numbers vary 'de + ou – 50 unités d'un jour sur l'autre',[37] an official euphemism for their frequency of the trains that take them to Auschwitz and almost certain gassing on arrival. In a dark and surreal dream, Cadin imagines these figures, recreating their voices as they sing out the word 'Pitchipoï', their name for the unknown destination. The dream also functions as a kaleidoscope of the many bloody incidents unearthed by Cadin's investigations. For in Cadin's disturbed sleep, the trains carrying the Jewish children from Drancy open to reveal the dead bodies of Algerian demonstrators. The horror of Cadin's dreamscape reminds the reader of the intersecting planes of guilt and responsibility that link historically distinct periods. Such crimes against humanity crystallize in the figure of André Veillut.

It is the voices of countless victims, such as the Jewish children, that impel Cadin to probe the recent past. Whilst others warn him off, he

---

[37] 'plus or minus fifty units from one day to the next'. Ibid. 179.

continues to express moral outrage at the crimes perpetrated in pursuit of the national interest. Targeting the high-ranking police official Veillut, Cadin is prepared to denounce the very institutions of which he is a representative. For Cadin ultimately places himself on the side of the victims and is not prepared to condone official compromises and omissions, unlike his colleague Dalbois who sacrifices truth for the sake of career advancement. Yet Cadin and Daeninckx are not naïve about the outcomes of such a stance. For if Cadin functions as a successful historian of sorts, sifting through the evidence, he has no illusions about the juridical mechanisms that will prevent the truth from coming out.

Veillut is murdered by Pierre Cazes, the secret agent who believed that he was acting in the national interest by killing Roger Thiraud on 17 October 1961. A form of justice has been meted out but, as the critic Pierre Verdaguer comments, it falls far short of what Cadin and the reader could have wished: 'car le monde ne se porte pas mieux de cette vengeance personnelle, dans la mesure où la justice n'a pas été rendue comme elle aurait dû l'être: devant les hommes, de façon exemplaire et purificatrice'.[38] For although Veillut has paid for his crimes with his life, his death does not serve the purposes of a wider social justice and is put down to personal vengeance by the authorities. Instead the public scrutiny of a trial has been avoided and an 'oubli juridique' (legal forgetting) ensures that state crimes against humanity are once again swept under the carpet.

In the epilogue to the text, Cadin and Claudine Chenet look on as an Algerian workman helps in the renovation of Bonne Nouvelle metro station. Tearing away layers of advertisements, the workman comes across a scarcely decipherable poster from the war years. This is revealed to be a German order banning assistance to Jews but remains only as half-formed words that must be recreated in the mind of the reader. Here, a wartime memory is recovered by a representative figure from another suppressed episode in French history. This image of the palimpsest highlights the centrality of the war years to contemporary French identity and its relationship to other narratives. Buried and overlaid with other memories, it remains at the core of that identity. Yet the active co-operation of the reader in making sense of that network of texts is an integral part of the process of remembering. *Meurtres pour mémoire* hammers this point home to the reader and impresses upon him or her the need for an active 'travail de mémoire' over admonitions to assume a more passive 'devoir

---

[38] 'because the world is no better as a result of this personal vengeance, to the extent that justice has not been done as it should have been: before others and in an exemplary and purifying manner'. Pierre Verdaguer, 'Les Tourments de l'enquêteur: Didier Daeninckx', in *La Séduction policière: signes de croissance d'un genre réputé mineur: Pierre Magnan, Daniel Pennac et quelques autres* (Birmingham, Ala.: Summa Publications, 1999), 233–70 (247).

de mémoire'.[39] The constant reactivation of a troubled past means confronting uncomfortable but necessary memories and guarding against collective amnesia. Constant vigilance, transparency, and open debate are the watchwords of the text and its message to French Republican society.

History, justice, fiction

Written during January and February 1983, *Meurtres pour mémoire* was, in many respects, to fulfil the well-worn mantra of life imitating art. In October 1997, Maurice Papon was tried for crimes against humanity. During the six-month trial, a jury was asked to decide on Papon's responsibility for the deportation of Jews from Bordeaux to Drancy. Controversy raged over the suitability of a courtroom as an arena in which to debate individual and collective knowledge of the Holocaust during the war years. Were not justice and history, although intersecting discourses in their search for truth, incompatible at many levels? Leading historians, such as Henry Rousso, claimed that sophisticated history findings were being manipulated for the partisan purposes of the juridical process. Tzetvan Todorov encapsulated many anxieties concerning the historical value of the trial when he contended that 'the courts are not a propitious source for the flowering of historical truth, for historical truth is not of the same nature as judicial truth, which recognizes only two values: guilt or innocence, black or white, yes or no'.[40] Faced with such a historic occasion, the jury found it impossible to rule decisively on such a complex set of issues

On 2 April 1998, Papon was found guilty of complicity in crimes against humanity and sentenced to ten years for his role in the arrest and detention of Jews. However, Papon was not found guilty of complicity in the murder of the Jewish deportees as the jury considered him to be ignorant of the final destination of the deportees. For many, the trial was a fudge of the basic issue of French state complicity in the Holocaust. Papon had been allowed to remain free throughout the trial on the grounds of ill health and when he absconded to Switzerland to avoid a court appearance for his appeal, it seemed that the state criminal would once again avoid his sanction. Recaptured, he successfully appealed against his

---

[39] 'memory work' and 'a duty to remember'. See the final sections of Charles Forsdick, 'Witnessing the Past in the French Polar', for an illuminating debate on the mechanisms of remembering and forgetting in Daeninckx's fiction.

[40] Todorov, 'Letter from Paris: The Papon Trial', in *Memory and Justice on Trial: The Papon Affair*, 217–22 (221).

conviction and was released from prison in September 2002 to the outrage of the families of his victims and many campaigners.

Other issues also surfaced at the trial, echoing the intersecting histories presented in *Meurtres pour mémoire*. For if Daeninckx chose not to untangle the convoluted connections between the war years and 17 October 1961, neither could the courtroom and the media. Even though the events of 17 October 1961 were not to be formally addressed at the trial, a 'virtual trial' outside the courtroom returned time and again to Papon's career as Paris Chief of Police in 1961 and his role in successive post-war administrations. Concluding that Papon was not an ideological fascist but more a representative of a certain class of French civil servants, the newspapers labelled his 'un crime de bureau' (an office crime), thereby condemning the systems and structures of the French State as much as its individual servants.

In prescient mode, *Meurtres pour mémoire* tackles many of the complex issues over history and retrospective justice that surfaced at the Papon trial. By focusing the murder inquiry on the character of a detective-historian, Daeninckx champions the work of the amateur and professional historian and highlights the mechanisms that prevent past secrets from coming to light. For even if the war criminal in *Meurtres pour mémoire* never reaches the courtroom and public sanction, it is due to the tireless efforts of intergenerational historians, such as Roger and Bernard Thiraud, that the truth finally emerges. Yet, such a victory is not the end of the story. History remains the site of a battle over French national identity in Daeninckx's novels.[41] In many of them, truth and reality are poised in a tense equilibrium where the role of fiction is to bring alternative histories to light and to challenge accepted versions of the past. As the opening quotation from Maurice G. Dantec makes clear, this can mean erecting fiction as a model of truth for all its mythologizing potential. *Meurtres pour mémoire* is one *roman noir* that takes this mission seriously, contesting the view that 'il ne sert à rien de revenir sur tous ces événements et de disséquer les responsabilités'.[42]

---

[41] See more recently Daeninckx's *Ethique en toc* (Paris: La Baleine, 2000) in which Daeninckx attacks the complacency of academic historians and implicates university authorities in the production and dissemination of work supporting the claims of Holocaust deniers.

[42] 'it serves no purpose to go back over events and to start analysing who is responsible'. Daeninckx, *Meurtres pour mémoire*, 116.

5 Telling Tales: Daniel Pennac, *La Fée Carabine* (1987)

L'idée que la lecture 'humanise l'homme' est juste dans son ensemble, même si elle souffre quelques déprimantes exceptions. On est sans doute un peu plus 'humain', entendons par là un peu plus solidaire de l'espèce [. . .] après avoir lu Tchekhov qu'avant.[1]

Immigration in post-war France

The 1980s represent a decade when immigration in France emerged as a political issue. Mainstream politicians shifted from considering the social and economic impact of successive waves of immigration towards a more ideologically defined estimation of immigration and its impact on French national identity. Such debates were influenced by the growing economic crisis that engulfed France in line with other Western democracies. During the 1980s, the decline in the nation's heavy industries, such as mining and shipbuilding, brought with it high levels of unemployment and a sense of social crisis. Such concerns seemed epitomized in the big state-subsidized housing estates on the periphery of many large cities, especially Paris. Reports of violence, racial tension, and disorder fuelled further anxieties about an impending social breakdown. Extreme right-wing political parties, such as the Front National, capitalized on such fears, making spurious claims that immigrant workers were one of the prime causes of the emerging economic crisis rather than its principle victims. Yet as social commentator Olivier Milza points out, scapegoating the immigrant population and their descendants is a well-rehearsed response to complex economic and social problems in twentieth-century France. For Milza, debates around immigration say more about a crisis in French identity than they do about the impact of immigration on life in contemporary France: 'l'immigration fonctionne aujourd'hui comme révélateur de la crise que traverse notre identité nationale'.[2]

---

[1] 'The idea that reading "humanizes man" is generally fair, even if it allows of a few depressing exceptions. We are probably a little more "human" and by that I mean we show a little more solidarity with the human race ... after having read Chekhov than before.' Daniel Pennac, *Comme un roman* (Paris: Gallimard, 1992), 168–9.

[2] 'Today, immigration functions as a means of revealing the crisis affecting our national identity.' Olivier Milza, *Les Français devant l'immigration* (Paris: Éditions Complexe, 1988), 16.

Post-war immigration was an integral part of the economic miracle that saw France transform itself into a modern, competitive, industrialized nation. From the 1940s through to the early 1970s, the French authorities welcomed a largely unskilled immigrant workforce into the country as a source of labour pivotal to the reconstruction of the French economy. In these years, the majority of such workers came from other European nations, such as Spain and Portugal. However, during and after the wars of decolonization in the 1950s and 1960s, such populations were supplemented by increasing numbers of workers arriving from former French colonies, particularly those in North Africa (Tunisia, Morocco, and Algeria). By the mid-1970s, the economic factors that had motivated the French government's immigration policies changed leading to a very different perception of immigrant communities in France.

In 1974, with the worsening international situation, particularly the oil crisis in the Middle East, the French government suspended its policies in favour of economic migration. This led to a dramatic drop in the number of immigrants entering France but did not tackle more insistent problems concerning the reception of immigrant communities into French society. By 1982, the African community was the majority immigrant population in France, accounting for just over 40 per cent of the total number. Concentrated on the outskirts of big cities, such communities tended to live in poor and deprived areas and survived on low incomes. Immigrant workers were over-represented in the unskilled industrial sector, the sector most at risk in times of economic instability, and were almost twice as likely to be unemployed as the majority population. The visibility of North African communities was heightened by cultural and religious differences that differentiated them from European immigrants. The presence of Islamic traditions and practices within a secular Republican culture became a hotly debated issue as critics and supporters argued over how and if the two cultures could coexist.[3]

In the early 1980s, the rising support for the Front National was one indicator of public receptiveness to more extremist views. Front National pronouncements on immigration, law and order, and unemployment made a causal link between minority populations and France's social and economic problems and their candidates made headway in local and European elections.[4] By the mid- to late 1980s, the debate over immigration in France had moved firmly to the right. From supporting the notion of 'le droit à la différence' (the right to difference), the Socialist

---

[3] See Jacques Voisard and Christiane Ducastelle, *La Question immigrée* (Paris: Calmann-Lévy, 1990) for an overview of public policy, as well as statistical data, relating to immigration in 1980s France.

[4] In 1984, the Front National gained 10.95% of the vote in European elections, with its greatest concentration of voters living in economically depressed regions of the country. See Milza, *Les Français devant l'immigration*, 68.

Party and other left-wing groupings espoused a Republican discourse on 'intégration' that underlined the duty of minority populations to adopt dominant French cultural norms.[5] The so called 'affaire du foulard' (headscarf affair) in 1989, when three Muslim schoolgirls wore head-scarves to school in defiance of the secular French school tradition, seemed to epitomize the clash of cultures many feared. Such events rein-forced the belief in many quarters that, in order to avoid social conflict, it was necessary to impose French traditions, even if this was at the risk of repressing the bicultural origins of many second-generation immigrant children.

Since its inception, the French *roman noir* has engaged with debates around immigration and national identity. Immigrant characters feature in some of the earliest French-authored *romans noirs*, such as André Piljean's *Passons la monnaie* (1951).[6] During the 1970s and early 1980s, a number of *roman noir* writers reflected more sensationalist visions of French city life that stigmatized immigrant communities as social out-casts.[7] Yet, in the best tradition of the *roman noir engagé*, in more recent years other writers have challenged such racist stereotypes and addressed the persecution and prejudice immigrants encounter on a daily basis. Jean-Bernard Pouy's *La Belle de Fontenay* (1992) is written from the view-point of an ageing Spanish political exile, Enric Jovillar, doubly marginal-ized by the fact that he is unable either to speak or to hear. Investigating the death of a young woman whose body was found on his allotment, Enric also comes to terms with his own flight from Spain escaping fascism. In Tonino Benacquista's *La Commedia des ratés* (1991), Antonio Polsinelli, a second-generation Italian immigrant, returns to Italy and his father's home village to solve the mystery of a friend's killing. Once again, the novel moves back in time to narrate the circumstances that brought Antonio's father to leave his native Italy. Daniel Pennac's series of comic detective novels, centring on the character of Benjamin Malaussène, also deals with the impact of immigration on French national identity. Immigrant characters may not be the main protagonists in the novel but,

---

[5] For a stimulating and informative discussion of ethnicity, identity, and the French Republican model, see David Blatt, 'Immigrant Politics in a Republican Nation', in Alec Hargreaves and Mark McKinney (eds.), *Post-Colonial Cultures in France* (London: Routledge, 1997), 40–55.

[6] André Piljean, *Passons la monnaie* (Paris: Gallimard, 1951) revolves around the police investigation of a money-counterfeiting ring during the Occupation. Political exiles from Spain and recent immi-grants from Algeria and Armenia provide the social backdrop for the action.

[7] Jean-Noël Blanc associates this *polar conservateur* with writers such as Raf Vallet, A. D. G., and Emmanuel Errer and discusses how such narratives pander to right-views fears of urban break down. See Jean-Noël Blanc, *Polarville: images de la ville dans le roman policier* (Lyon: Presses Universitaires de Lyon, 1991), part 3, ch. 3, 'La Ville envahie, la ville perdue'.

in *La Fée Carabine* (1987) the second in the series, Pennac confronts not only present-day racism but also the heritage of France's colonial past. In so doing, the novel proposes a utopian social vision that embraces multiculturalism.

The 'post-literary novel': French fiction in the 1980s

In recent years, literary critics have discussed the 1980s and early 1990s as signalling a significant shift in French literary practices. For Colin Nettelbeck, these years witnessed the decline of the novel as the dominant force in French cultural life and an upsurge in other artistic forms and media, like film.[8] A number of novelists in the 1980s took on board such changing public tastes, producing novels that drew on a variety of cultural influences in a knowing and self–referential way. Nettelbeck describes this hybrid literary form as the 'post-literary novel', a term that 'designates not the demise of the literary, but the displacement of a cultural dominant, and the relativization of what had been a quasi-absolute social value'.[9] For Nettelbeck, the contemporary novel in recent years has detached itself from its reputation as a privileged conduit for French thought. Selected novelists have revitalized form and content with an injection of popular culture adapted from sources such as detective fiction, science fiction, and the *bande dessinée*. Authors, such as Daniel Pennac, Jean Echenoz, and Patrick Modiano, no longer consider it their role to produce the great literary epic but rather to delight and entertain.

According to Nettelbeck, the reasons for such changing patterns in French fiction can be attributed to both long-term historical trends and more recent developments in post-war French literary life. For Nettelbeck, the pace of modernization in France from the end of the nineteenth century onwards has affected the status of the novel and canonical French literature as whole. The secularization of French society brought with it a loss of faith in the written word to express the great truths of the day, imaged most powerfully in the fractured modernist texts of the turn of the century. In more recent years, the importance of French as a language has been challenged by the rise of English as the global means of communication. No longer the medium of international culture and diplomacy,

---

[8] Colin Nettelbeck, 'The "Post-Literary" Novel: Echenoz, Pennac and Company', *French Cultural Studies*, 5/2 (1994), 111–38.   [9] Ibid. 115.

French has had to carve out a different path for itself, best illustrated by organized efforts to support a worldwide community of French speakers known as *francophonie*.

The French literary establishment too has played its part in the decline of the novel as a form. The *nouveau roman* in the 1950s and 1960s challenged the primacy of staple features of the novel such as plot and character, emphasizing instead literary experimentation and the subversion of traditional notions of structure and narration. Into the post-1968 period, such challenges to conventional forms were taken further as theorists developed models of literary criticism that deconstructed the text and threw out the notion of authorial intention. Interpreting the novel as a network of systems and signs led to the treatment of individual works as segments of narrative to be dissected and analysed.

The post-literary novels of Pennac, Echenoz, and others can be read on one level as an attempt to break free from such high theory and to re-engage with the everyday reader. Part of this process entails revisiting well-established genres and forms of writing, such as detective fiction, but with what Charles Porter has called 'a cool, ironic detachment' that plays with reader expectations and assumptions.[10] Above all, the post-literary novelists insist on the power of narrative and the primacy of storytelling. As Elizabeth Fallaize and Colin Davis have commented, this return to storytelling was an important aspect of French fiction in the Mitterrand years (1981–95).[11] Writing and reading are imagined as acts of seduction that give the pleasure of immersion in an identifiable and entertaining fictional universe.

Pennac's Malaussène novels revolve obsessively around storytelling and its multiple functions. Yet telling tales is not always a fanciful or positive symbol of the times in his novels. Telling tales is also about attempting to impose order and coherence on the chaos of life where loss, absence, and death are daily occurrences. As an example of the post-literary novel, Pennac's work shows up more acutely than perhaps any other writer of the decade the interaction of high and popular culture. Initially published in the Série noire, Pennac's phenomenal rise to fame led to his publication in more prestigious collections. His special brand of the *roman noir* catapulted him into the literary mainstream and fuelled debates on the cross-fertilization of *littérature noire* (crime fiction) and *littérature blanche* (mainstream fiction).

---

[10] Charles Porter, Foreword to 'After the Age of Suspicion: The French Novel Today', *Yale French Studies*, (1988), 1–4 (3).

[11] Colin Davis and Elizabeth Fallaize, 'Introduction' to *French Fiction in the Mitterrand Years: Memory, Narrative, Desire* (Oxford: Oxford University Press, 2000), 1–17 (15).

The Pennac phenomenon

The son of a career army officer, Daniel Pennac spent much of his youth abroad in South-East Asia and Africa and trained as a teacher on his return to France. In provocative fashion, his first publication was a polemical essay on military service to be followed by two novels that met with little commercial success. After a period abroad, Pennac returned to France and wrote three children's books before embarking on *Au bonheur des ogres* (1985). Published in the Série noire, the novel became an international best-seller. However, Pennac's time as a Série noire writer was short-lived. After the second of the Malaussène novels, *La Fée Carabine* (1987), Pennac switched to Gallimard's mainstream collection and was awarded the Prix Inter for the third novel in the series *La Petite Marchande de prose* (1989). With six novels in the series to date,[12] Pennac has been fêted as a publishing phenomenon drawing readers of all ages into his humorous and highly idiosyncratic chronicle of family life in the multi-ethnic district of Belleville in Paris. With their mix of social realism and fairytale elements, Pennac's Malaussène novels defy easy categorization. Some, like Patrick Raynal, current editor of the Série noire, dispute the *roman noir* label, claiming that Pennac's novels rely on a personal realm of play and fantasy rather than the conventions of the *roman noir*.[13] However, this is to ignore the hybrid nature of Pennac's production. His comic mystery novels have affinities with pre-war French detective fiction, as well as with the classic American *roman noir*.

In his study of detective fiction, Francis Lacassin devotes five of the fourteen chapters to French writers, one of whom is Pierre Véry.[14] Lacassin's comments on Véry are illuminating as they highlight a pre-war tradition of French detective fiction that drew on *noir*-like elements of the baroque and the gothic. Lacassin examines Véry's detective fiction as blurring the boundaries between the real and fantasy, uncovering the magical qualities of the everyday. Dreams, premonitions, and superstitions play an important part in the narrative and mysteries are resolved less by an act of logical deduction than through deciphering textual

---

[12] The six volumes to date are *Au bonheur des ogres* (1985), *La Fée Carabine* (1987), *La Petite Marchande de prose* (1989), *Monsieur Malaussène* (1995), *Des chrétiens et des maures* (1996), and *Aux fruits de la passion* (1999), as well as a one-man play, *Monsieur Malaussène* (1996).

[13] In interview, Raynal described Pennac's publication in the Série noire as something of an 'accident', precipitated by himself and Jean-Bernard Pouy with whom Pennac had already collaborated on *La Vie Duraille* (Paris: Éditions Fleuve noir, 1985), published under the name J.-B. Nacray. Interview with Raynal, Paris, 13 February 2002.

[14] Francis Lacassin, *Mythologie du roman policier* (Paris: UGE, 1974), 41–113.

conundrums. This is perhaps best illustrated by *Le Testament de Basil Crookes* (1930) which tells the tale of Basil Crookes, a failed writer, who declares in a letter that if a copy of his failed work and his letter are reunited a reward will be made available to the happy winner.[15] Murder, mayhem, and intrigue ensue as characters in the Highlands of Scotland battle to be the first to do this. Eventually, when testament and book are reunited the prize is revealed to be an engraving and the injunction not to follow the author's example and to refrain from writing literature.

In many ways, Pennac's Malaussène series can be read as reviving this pre-war comic mystery tradition. The Malaussène children (and their dog Julius) have a gift for predicting the future and perform poetic transformations on the world around them. Fairytale and mythical archetypes jostle for space with clichés of popular culture, while word games and the act of storytelling direct the action. Like Véry, Pennac sets out to test the limits of the detective fiction format, deliberately constructing his novels as a subversion of conventional genre rules and playing with images and intrigues focused on literary production. Yet for all their game-playing, the early Malaussène novels, particularly the first two published in the Série noire, remain firmly wedded to the urban setting and themes of the *roman noir*: the city at night, a bloody series of murders, the involvement of the police, especially Chief Superintendent Coudrier, and the designation of Benjamin Malaussène as the prime suspect. Such elements are instantly recognizable to the reader and their reworking is part of the pleasure of the text. For Pennac's attraction to the *roman noir* format is centred on its narrative possibilities and its popular appeal as a modern-day epic of the city. As his essay on reading, *Comme un roman* (1992), makes clear, one of the motivations for his writing is to celebrate the power of literature and its relevancy to modern life.

Comme un roman is an imaginative meditation on the pleasures of reading, as well as a serious attempt to diagnose why and how children lose their initial love of books and storytelling. It begins, fable-like, with the story of a schoolboy shut up in his bedroom at home trying to wade his way through the class assignment, a weighty nineteenth-century tome; each time he opens the book, he falls asleep at page 48. The injunction to read has had the reverse effect and made reading a chore rather then a pleasure. Where, the essay asks, has the love of reading gone? How can it be resuscitated? For the narrator, the solution lies in changing the child's perception of reading. Most important of all is the necessity to reconnect with an oral tradition of storytelling which demands the participation of the child's parents. Moving away from an obsessive concern with

---

[15] Véry's novel won the Prix du roman d'aventures in 1930.

academic grades and critical analysis liberates the child reader and leads to an unqualified immersion in fiction of all kinds.

In *Comme un roman*, Pennac challenges readers' perceptions of books. They are not sacred objects of French culture and readers are assigned 'rights' rather than duties, such as the right not to read to the end of the book or to skip pages. Reading is for pleasure and, although the narrator peppers his essay with references to the great works of European culture, Kafka, Mann, Shakespeare, Dostoevsky, his appeal to read is directed at all literature. In the essay, re-engaging with literature and books is above all about satisfying our need for stories, narratives that tell the reader something about themselves and the world around them. For though the narrator may not hammer home his message in overtly didactic terms, it is clear that storytelling has many positive personal and collective benefits. It is a moment of intimacy and communion between the storyteller and her/his listeners; it brings relief and comfort as a temporary respite in hard times; and it offers the reader a reflection or meditation on their own times and that of other cultures. All these themes come to the fore in *La Fée Carabine*, the second in the Malaussène series of novels. Published as a Série noire title, this book illustrates perhaps more than any other book in the series, Pennac's indebtedness to the *roman noir* format. The novel is also a deeply politicized vision of contemporary France and challenges many of the racist stereotypes of the 1980s. As a point of intersection between comedy, *roman noir*, and politics, *La Fée Carabine* stands as a good example of Pennac's unique brand of *noir* narrative.

La Fée Carabine: 'imposer le sérieux par le comique'

The convoluted plot of *La Fée Carabine* revolves around the modern drug trade but in totally unexpected ways. For in the narrative, it emerges that old people living in areas of Paris undergoing redevelopment have been hooked on drugs to hasten their deaths. This allows a conglomerate of vested interests to acquire their apartments at vastly reduced prices and make huge profits. This real-estate scandal and its human cost is exacerbated by the reign of terror of a serial killer in Belleville who slits the throats of old women in their homes at night to feed his drug habit. Related to these events is the killing of a racist policeman, Vanini, in the opening pages of the novel. This plot summary, however, misses out the wonderful exuberance of the novel and its colourful cast of characters. The main focus of the text is the Malaussène family, an assortment of half-brothers and -sisters who live in the Belleville district of Paris in an unconventional extended family unit that includes a cohort of little old men. The latter are former drug addicts saved by the compassion and caring of the Malaussène children. As the novel progresses, the chief suspect in the police investigation of murder and drug trafficking becomes Benjamin Malaussène, the oldest brother and nominal head of the family.

Ben's vocation in life as a scapegoat means that he acts as a magnet for all the criminal activities that erupt in the novel. His networks of relations connect him to the investigative journalist Julie Corrençon, on the trail of the drug pushers until they torture her and leave her for dead; to the Hadouch family who are wrongly suspected of drug running and murdering Vanini; and to the publishing house Éditions du Talion who are to publish a glossy album by the architect, Ponthard-Delmaire, the figure at the heart of the real-estate swindle. Such an implausible set of coincidences make even Malaussène's ally, Chief Superintendent Coudrier, sigh to his junior colleague, Pastor: 'tentative de meurtre, trafic de drogues, assassinats réitérés, en fait de soupçons, ce n'est pas un suspect que vous tenez là, c'est une anthologie!'[16] Elements of the marvellous and fantastical are set alongside a dark vision of contemporary urban life. It is the interpenetration of these two worlds that enables Pennac to 'imposer le sérieux par le comique'.[17]

The fictional universe of *La Fée Carabine* is one that depicts a world in crisis. The ideal of the extended Malaussène family is contrasted to a strong sense of social breakdown. Characters are depicted as isolated and adrift, grieving for the death of loved ones. The main police figures in the text, Pastor and Van Thian, are lonely figures, parentless and victim to bouts of depression. The pervasive presence of drugs in the narrative is not only a motor for action but also a metaphor for a social order that is in need of the medically assisted consolation it affords. Not only are the grandfathers adopted by the Malaussène family former addicts, but others too rely to varying degrees on substance abuse to see them through the day. Van Thian is constantly popping pills and the misuse of drugs in hospital treatment is highlighted in Julie's case as her surgeon keeps her in a drug-induced coma to save her an apparently traumatic recovery. Drugs symbolize the atomized and fractured existence of many characters in the book who fear that they have no future.

---

[16] 'Suspicion of attempted murder, drug trafficking, serial killing, you haven't got a suspect there but a catalogue of crimes!' Daniel Pennac, *La Fée Carabine* (Paris: Gallimard, 1987), 182. The novel has been translated as *The Fairy Gunmother* by Ian Monk (London: Harvill Press, 1997).

[17] 'to use comedy to make a serious point'. Taken from Kirsten Halling and Roger Célestin, 'Interview with Daniel Pennac: The Writer's Trade, Detective Fiction, and Popular Culture', *Sites*, 1/1 (Spring 1997), 333–47 (337).

In *La Fée Carabine*, the reasons for such a breakdown in social relations are related to the failure, absence, and death of a number of founding fathers. Contemporary French society in the novel is a strangely apatriarchal culture, either bereft of positive authority figures or reliant on corrupt ones. It is significant that fathers play no part in the Malaussène family unit, as the mother's flings with various men result in numerous offspring but no discernible input from the progenitors. In clearly symbolic mode, other lost fathers relate to major developments in post-war France. Pastor's adopted father, The Councillor, was the founder of the French welfare state. With the novel dedicated to 'la Sécu', the French social security system, it is no surprise that such a figure is an emblem of disinterested humanism. Yet perhaps the most significant founding father in the text is Jean-Baptiste Corrençon, fêted as the architect of post-war French decolonization.

Corrençon is the father of Julie Corrençon, Ben's lover and the investigative journalist who discovers the collusion of big business (architect, Ponthard-Delmaire), the police (narcotics squad leader, Cercaire) and the State (Minister for Senior Citizens, Armand Le Capelier) in the drugs scandal. In classic *roman noir* mode, Julie reveals the corrupt underbelly of metropolitan French life. Yet Julie's motivations are neither political nor ethical but linked to her personal battle against opium addiction, her father's killer. Julie's childhood memories of her father's opium addiction are a source of great pain and distress. For Jean-Baptiste's drug habit is accelerated by a desperate sense of disenchantment as the former colonial governor who engineered French decolonization. After the euphoria of liberation, the fratricidal battles that took place between former friends and allies whom he had helped to independence ravages Jean-Baptiste's physical and mental health: 'ce n'étaient plus ses propres contradictions qu'il traquait dans ses veines, mais celles du monde qu'il avait contribué à faire naître. A peine les Indépendances proclamées, la Géographie engendrait l'Histoire, comme une maladie incurable. Une épidémie qui laissait des cadavres.'[18] The human cost of decolonization in death, disaster, and population displacement is realized in the drugs-related death of a humanitarian leader and visionary.

La Fée Carabine confronts the consequences of post-war decolonization and its impact on French national identity in a number of ways. Firstly, it addresses the issue of immigration and the identity crisis of second-generation children. The conflict at the heart of such hybrid cultural origins is represented most poignantly in the character of Van Thian, the half

---

[18] 'It was no longer his own contradictions that he chased in his veins but those of a world that he had helped to create. No sooner had a series of colonial independences been proclaimed, than Geography engendered History like an incurable disease. An epidemic that left many dead bodies.' Pennac, *La Fée Carabine*, 284.

French, half Vietnamese policeman who dresses up as the Widow Hô, in order to catch the Belleville serial killer. This disguise, envisaged as bait for the killer, transforms into a comic manifestation of the struggles faced by second-generation children to be accepted fully by either culture.[19] As he lies in his hospital bed with bullet wounds, the double personality of Van Thian and Widow Hô battle for control of his soul: 'L'inspecteur Van Thian partageait son lit avec une veuve vietnamienne, la veuve Hô. Prisonniers du même corps, la veuve et l'inspecteur semblaient instruire le même divorce depuis une éternité.'[20] Like a squabbling married couple, each accuses the other of misrepresenting or suppressing the other's existence in an image of irreconcilable difference. The novel asks, how can one adopt a French identity that does not at the same time acknowledge powerful influences linked to family and religion? As an image of the continuing conflict at the heart of French national identity, the character of Van Thian raises the spectre of a whole generation's alienation from their bicultural origins.

Another consequence of France's bloody colonial history envisaged in the book is racism. The novel begins with the police officer, Vanini, watching an old lady cross an icy road. His narrative perspective dominates as he imagines the sheet of ice she crosses to be a map of Africa: 'A force de progression reptante, ses charentaises l'avaient menée, disons, jusqu'au milieu du Sahara, sur la plaque à forme d'Afrique.'[21] For Vanini, Africa remains an abstracted land mass, not a continent of real people. His perception of the old lady inching slowly across the ice sheet is a fantasized and nostalgic vision of French colonial possession and mastery. Vanini's thoughts, as reported by the narrator, show up all the fundamental misrepresentations of immigration that characterized extreme right-wing views in 1980s France: 'Il était Frontalement National, le blondinet, *en sorte qu'*il avait eu à réfléchir objectivement sur les dangers de l'immigration sauvage; et il avait conclu, en tout bon sens, qu'il fallait les virer vite fait, tous ces crouilles, rapport à la pureté du cheptel français d'abord, au chômage ensuite, et à la sécurité enfin.'[22] Vanini trots out the well-worn

---

[19] See Jean-Xavier Ridon's 'Mémoire, récit et contamination dans *La Fée Carabine* de Daniel Pennac', *L'Esprit créateur*, 37/3 (Autumn 1997), 50–60 (51–2) for a discussion of Belleville as emblematic of a France in search of a multicultural identity.

[20] 'Inspector Van Thian was sharing his bed with a Vietnamese widow, the Widow Hô. Imprisoned within the same body, the widow and the inspector seemed to have been in the throes of divorce proceedings for an eternity.' Pennac, *La Fée Carabine*, 300.

[21] 'By dint of crawling progress, her slippers had taken her to the middle of the Sahara, let's say, on the sheet of ice shaped like Africa.' Pennac, *La Fée Carabine*, 13.

[22] 'He was Nationally Frontal, the blond-haired lad, as a consequence of having thought objectively about the dangers of unchecked immigration and he had sensibly concluded that they needed to get rid of all that scum double quick. First, to maintain the purity of French livestock, then because of unemployment and lastly to uphold law and order.' Pennac, *La Fée Carabine*, 14.

themes on immigration, unemployment, and law and order. Such views are comically undercut when he is shot at point-blank range by the little old lady, mistaking him for the Belleville serial killer as he comes to her aid.

This comic treatment of the main racist figure does not detract, however, from sinister and more troubling aspects of racism in the text. The arrest of Hadouch as a suspected drugs dealer points to police persecution of North African immigrants in their search for the guilty party. As an immigrant, Hadouch makes a convenient scapegoat and conforms to widespread prejudices in the novel that drugs are necessarily being peddled and used by the immigrant youth of Belleville. As the novel makes clear, it is at the other end of the age spectrum that the police should be looking. However, Hadouch's persecution is no arbitrary case. He is harassed, beaten, and hospitalized for photographs in his possession that show Vanini brutally attacking North African demonstrators. Apart from the more cerebral figures of Van Thian, Pastor, and Coudrier, the police are depicted as a bunch of homicidal thugs, taken in by simplistic solutions to complex problems. As in other books in the Malaussène series, however, their suspicions eventually fall on Ben, the fall guy for the crimes (and sins) of others.

One of the most striking comic features of *La Fée Carabine* is the presence of Benjamin Malaussène as the 'bouc emissaire' or scapegoat for the whole community. As Colin Davis and Elizabeth Fallaize have discussed, this image draws on the work of René Girard and a mythic interpretation of the scapegoat as the figure who allows the community to exculpate itself at times of crisis.[23] By projecting collective feelings of guilt and anxiety onto a representative figure, often linked to a minority grouping of some kind, the community cleanses itself of all association with evil or disaster. In the fictional universe of the Malaussène novels, Ben is just such a figure. He begins in *Au bonheur des ogres* (1985) working in a department store in the fictitious position of 'Technical Inspector' where his real role is to take the blame when customers return to complain of faulty items. His compassion, sense of concern, and humanity disarm the complainants and save the store money. In *La Fée Carabine*, he is working for the publishing house Éditions du Talion in an equally thankless role, employed to take the wrath of disappointed and angry would-be novelists. Yet, as his boss la Reine Zabo counters when Ben asks for extended holidays, his job is more than a profession, it is a vocation and is not confined to office hours. He cannot escape his fate as the community's

---

[23] See Colin Davis and Elizabeth Fallaize, 'Detective Fictions: Daniel Pennac's *Au bonheur des ogres*', in *French Fiction in the Mitterrand Years*, 37–60.

scapegoat: '*n'imaginez pas que vous cessez d'être Bouc Emissaire parce que vous prenez des vacances!* Bouc, vous l'êtes jusque dans la moelle de vos os. Tenez, si en ce moment même on cherche le responsable d'une grosse connerie dans la ville, vous avez toutes les chances d'être désigné!'[24] And this is precisely what happens.

The catalogue of crimes attributed to Ben reaches gigantic proportions and much of the comedy of the narrative comes from his unwitting implication in a series of bloody murders. For friends and family, he is a latter-day saint in his quest to protect them from the horrors of the outside world. Yet in the spiritual void of the text, the saintly Ben is a fallible creation racked with doubt and uncertainty and often poorly placed to save those for whom he cares. He is a pitiable detective, regularly mistaking the murderer and his motivations, and is only cleared of criminal charges thanks to a combination of chance, fate, and good luck. Throughout his misadventures, narratives and storytelling are pivotal to the action. It is telling tales that saves the day.

The fictional universe of Pennac's Malaussène novels is saturated in references to literary production of all sorts. The titles of the first three books in the series highlight the formal hybridity of his series and the comic value inherent in juxtaposing narratives of reality and fantasy. *Au bonheur des ogres* reworks the title of Zola's nineteenth-century tale of a Parisian department store, *Au bonheur des dames* (1883) with a fairytale spin. *La Fée Carabine* merges the *la fée carabosse*, the bad fairy of legends, with the guns and rifles ('carabine') of the *roman noir* world. *La Petite Marchande de prose* plays on the figure of Hans Christian Anderson's little match girl, here elided with the world of publishing. In *La Fée Carabine*, Pennac takes the intersection of these worlds further as characters are imagined in a series of archetypal fairytale roles: as she lies in her coma, Julie becomes Sleeping Beauty needing the kiss of her Prince Charming to awaken her from her slumbers; Thérese is the sorceress capable of predicting the future; while the 'fée carabosse/carabine' is the little old lady of the opening pages who is metamorphosed into a fairy in the fertile imagination of one of Ben's brothers, Le Petit, when he witnesses her killing Vanini.

Added to the complicity of these worlds are other layers of reference that make for the rich cultural mix of Pennac's text. Literary classics are the stuff of gripping bedtime reading, as grandfather Risson brings alive Tolstoy's *War and Peace*. Yet the novel is also suffused with knowing

---

[24] 'Don't think that you stop being the Scapegoat because you're on holiday! You are a goat to the very core of your being. You know, if just now they are looking for the person responsible for some great foul-up in town, you are the most likely person to be picked out!' Pennac, *La Fée Carabine*, 24.

asides to popular culture, such as Belgian cartoon strips, Spanish detective fiction (Manuel Vásquez Montalbán's Pepe Carvalho) and TV films. These contribute to the cinematic quality of the prose, as for example when Pastor enters the police station after discovering Julie Corrençon, fortuitously rescued from drowning by a passing barge when she is thrown unconscious from a bridge. The ensuing scene reads like the stage directions of every cop show ever seen: 'Pastor retrouva la Maison en éruption: couloir bondés d'Arabes assis par terre ou serrés sur des bancs, claquements de porte, coups de gueules, sonneries de téléphone, rafles de machines à écrire, va-et-vient de dossiers à grandes enjambées de flics furibards . . .'.[25] This sea of cultural references is further magnified by the multiple functions storytelling fulfils in the narrative.

Telling tales is first a means of making sense of the chaotic world that engulfs the characters.[26] The Malaussène children are unstinting in their clamour for bedtime stories. Every event or episode is grist to the mill so that by the end of the novel Van Thian, the newly elected storyteller, is telling the children the story of the 'fée carabine' in a parodic image of the 'book within a book' formula. However, storytelling does not take place only in such familiar domesticated settings and it is not the exclusive preserve of children. Stories and adventures of all kinds are recounted in the novel. Most show up the insecurities, fears, and desires of Belleville's inhabitants. The best illustration of this are the stories swapped by Pastor and Van Thian every night in their shared office. Some are taken from police reports or accounts of their childhood, others are humorous anecdotes, proverbs, or vignettes of daily life.

In this context, telling tales is a comfort and protection that allows the policemen to digest the horrors they witness on a daily basis. After interrogating hardened criminals, Pastor usually returns a shadow of his former self, completely drained by the experience. It is at these moments that Van Thian 'resuscitates' him with entertaining stories. These modern-day 'tales of the city' deliberately undercut the grandiose ambitions of the epic sagas of antiquity. Instead they are more modest tales that give a jaundiced but amused insight into prevalent social and cultural mores. One of the best example is the tale of the rock climber recounted by Van Thian. A rock climber has an accident and is left hanging from a icy ledge of granite looking over a 2,000 metre fall. The climber calls out for help: 'Et Dieu reprend: "Si tu as confiance en Moi, lâche cette foutue plate-forme, Je

[25] 'Pastor found the Station in chaos: there were corridors crammed full of Arabs sitting on the floor or squeezed onto benches, doors slamming, people shouting, phones ringing, bursts of typewriters, hopping mad cops striding this way and that with files . . .'. Pennac, *La Fée Carabine*, 55.
[26] For an illuminating analysis of the functions of storytelling along these lines in the Malaussène novels, see David J. Bond, 'Daniel Pennac: des Histoires d'histoires', *LittéRéalité*, 10/2 (1998), 53–60.

t'envoie deux anges qui te rattraperont en plein vol . . ." Le petit alpiniste
réfléchit un instant, puis, dans le silence redevenu sidéral, il demande: "Y
a quelqu'un d'autre?" '[27] Van Thian's story underlines the secular beliefs
at the heart of Pennac's writing. Grand narratives of faith, hope, and
salvation have no place in this world pervaded by a more mundane sense
of fear, uncertainty, and indecision. Yet if the rock climber cannot believe
in the divine power of God, his audacious reply shows he has not given up
believing in the assistance of his fellow men.

   Telling tales is equally about promoting social cohesion. As Colin Davis
and Elizabeth Fallaize note: 'storytelling performs the crucial function in
Pennac's novels of binding together in something like a unified community a selection of listeners who otherwise have little in common'.[28]
Adopted grandfathers, children, family, and friends are all reconciled in
the ritual of the bedtime story initially narrated by Risson, the former
department-store book salesman who appears in *Au bonheur des ogres*. As
in *Comme un roman*, storytelling operates as 'un moment de communion
[. . .] un retour au seul paradis qui vaille: l'intimité'.[29] Yet, this thirst for
stories has its downside. Telling tales can lead to misinterpretations and
misreadings. In *La Fée Carabine*, Pastor himself plays on the narrative
sensibilities of his criminal opponents, Cercaire and Ponthard-Delmaire,
to persuade them that he can create a convincing story implicating Ben
in all their misdemeanours. Telling tales can also lead to deception and
duplicity, framing others for crimes they did not commit. This is the case
with the police, happy to fabricate an identity for Hadouch as a drugs
dealer so that he will hand over photos incriminating Vanini in police
violence. Yet perhaps the most gruesome and bloody consequence of
storytelling in the book is murder.

   In the most implausible explanation of all, storytelling is the motivation
for murder. Risson executes his victims in order to buy drugs that will
enable him to bring literature back to life for the Malaussène children
and their bedtime stories: 'Ces romans dorment et il me faut, chaque fois,
les réveiller. Une petite piqûre est alors indispensable. C'est à cela que
j'utilise l'argent de ces veuves incultes: pour acheter de quoi réveiller la
Littérature dans mes veines afin d'illuminer l'esprit de ces enfants.'[30] This

---

[27] 'And God replies: "If you believe in me, let go of that bloody ledge. I will send you two angels and
they will catch you as you fall…" The little rock climber thinks for a minute, then, in the void of
silence, he asks again: "Is there anyone else?"' Pennac, *La Fée Carabine*, 196.
[28] Davis and Fallaize, *French Fiction in the Mitterrand Years*, 15.
[29] Pennac, *Comme un roman*, 36.
[30] 'These novels are sleeping and each time I have to wake them up. A little injection is indispensable
for this. That's how I use these uneducated widows' money; to buy something to set literature
coursing through my veins so that I can enlighten the minds of those children.' Pennac, *La Fée
Carabine*, 244–5.

defence is laughable and yet strangely alluring. Storytelling here is no peripheral activity in life but the lifeblood of the community for which murder can be contemplated. Risson is a despicable character from many angles with his right-wing and anti-Semitic comments.[31] Yet he is also a pitiable figure, seeking out a role for himself as storyteller in a world that has cast him on the rubbish heap once retired. His dedication to story-telling remains after his death. Van Thian takes his place as the family storyteller in a narrative continuum that saves the children from the inva-sion of television and gathers them together as a community of readers and listeners.

Social visions

La Fée Carabine combines social realism with the magical and fairytale in its quest to represent life in contemporary France. The social vision that it provides its readers is one that some have seen as utopian for its depiction of a harmonious multi-ethnic and multicultural community in Belleville. The Malaussène 'tribe' is welcoming of others, irrespective of age or ethnic origin, and shows a compassionate concern for the excluded that can make Ben and his siblings appear like an updated version of care in the community. This vision has a political purpose. Images of adolescents as juvenile delinquents, immigrants as criminals, and old-age pensioners as perennial victims create stereotypes. As Pennac himself explained in interview, La Fée Carabine was conceived as a deliberate attempt to 'tourner des stéréotypes, pas un, mais tous de façon absolument systéma-tique', to reconfigure what others accepted as the status quo.[32] In the novel, it is the multicultural youth of Belleville who protect the old ladies and solve the mysterious identity of the serial killer of geriatrics, not the police. The State is presented as criminal in the person of the Minister for Senior Citizens, Armand Le Capelier, one of the masterminds behind the drugs trade. In a fictional universe when state-run organizations fail to protect and provide, community networks take their place.

Although some may consider this social vision to be simplistic and even blinkered when faced with the current rise of drug addiction and crime in many French and Western urban centres, Pennac's fictional universe

---

[31] Colin Nettelbeck makes the point that Risson is a play on Robert Faurisson—fau(x) risson—an infamous academic Holocaust denier who came to prominence in France in the 1980s. See 'The "Post-Literary" Novel: Echenoz, Pennac and Company', 133.

[32] 'Interview avec Didier Daeninckx et Daniel Pennac', Quebec français, 72 (December 1988), 74–5 (74).

does ask some penetrating questions about who is responsible for a sense of social crisis in the cities, who can be judged the guilty party, and who are the victims. The well-worn tale of the immigrant community as the cause of pervasive socio-economic problems is quashed and their scapegoating is condemned as a convenient 'tale' that assuages ingrained French fears and anxieties. By focusing on a long-term history of French immigration, including the wars of decolonization, Pennac asks the reader to look beyond the media hype and the propaganda of the Far Right to see how interconnected France and its former colonies are. As a melting pot of cultures and identities, the world of *La Fée Carabine* is offered up as an example of the benefits of immigration and the integral part minority communities play in social cohesion. As the opening quotation in this chapter makes clear, Pennac believes storytelling and reading contribute to this process, sensitizing readers to others' plights and encouraging a sense of solidarity with fellow human beings. In *La Fée Carabine*, 'imposer le sérieux par le comique' is precisely to use the comic resources of the novel for a serious message about the power of literature to promote a more tolerant society.

6 Feminist Fictions:
Maud Tabachnik, *Un été pourri* (1994)

Parce que si les femmes qui écrivent des romans noirs prennent de plus en plus de place dans la littérature du même couleur, c'est peut-être que l'on s'avise que notre société qui s'était contentée jusque-là d'une vision essentiellement masculine, [. . .] avait besoin d'être analysée et racontée par l'autre moitié.[1]

Women, feminism, parity

Since 1945, women in France, and in Western Europe more generally, have made significant breakthroughs in areas such as civil and political rights, control over their bodies, paid work, and education.[2] The post-war period in France opened with the momentous decision to grant French women the right to vote and to stand as candidates in nationwide elections. In the first post-war legislative elections held in October 1945, thirty-five women were returned as deputies to the French National Assembly. Over the post-war era, major legislation has been introduced that has revolutionized women's lives, such as the decriminalization of abortion and the right to contraception.[3] Yet despite such obvious advances, France still remains a deeply patriarchal society where influential institutions, such as the judiciary, are male-dominated. Economic, social, and political inequalities persist in areas such as equal pay, and the glass ceiling remains a reality for many working women who juggle domestic responsibilities and career development.

Yet in terms of women's awareness of gender issues, the post-war era has witnessed the erosion of many stereotypes and taboos. The rise of

---

[1] 'Because if women who write romans noirs are increasingly finding a place in literature of the same colour, it is perhaps because we are suddenly realizing that our society, which until now had been content with an essentially masculine vision, [...] needed to be analysed and recounted by the other half.' Maud Tabachnik, 'Remarques sur la non-place des femmes dans le roman noir', *Les Temps modernes*, 595 (1997), 122–9 (128).

[2] For a stimulating set of essays on aspects of women's lives in contemporary France, see Abigail Gregory and Ursula Tidd (eds), *Women in Contemporary France* (Oxford: Berg, 2000).

[3] Contraception was legalized in 1967 and abortion in 1975 with the cost of the operation reimbursable through the state social security system from 1983.

second-wave feminism gave many French women the intellectual tools
with which to examine their social and political condition. Simone de
Beauvoir's *Le Deuxième sexe*, first published in 1949, is a seminal text for
its investigation of woman as the relative 'other' to the universal male
subject of Western culture. Beauvoir analyses various aspects of women's
oppression in society and her work was to strike a chord with a generation
of women struggling to understand their position in post-war France.
Whilst women activists continued to campaign on a variety of issues over
the 1950s and 1960s, it was the events of May 1968 that signalled a sea-
change in French feminism. Men and women fought side by side against
what they perceived to be a moribund social and political order. Yet for
many women, these heady days of social and political protest also led to a
growing realization that the revolutionary models and concepts of their
fellow male activists largely excluded considerations of gender.

In the aftermath of events of May 1968, French feminists, influenced
particularly by the Women's Liberation Movement in America, developed
autonomous groups to discuss questions of sexual difference and equality.[4] French feminism was by no means a united or homogenous movement and dissent and conflict characterized its development over the
1970s and early 1980s. Some activists argued for sexual difference and
the specificity of a feminine identity that was associated with 'écriture
féminine', a poetic sensibility that draws on the rhythms of the body and
celebrates motherhood. Others worked more closely with the material
inequalities that oppressed women in patriarchal society. A third grouping aligned feminism with the class struggle and French socialism. Of
those who focused on the socio-economic factors in women's oppression, a number were prepared to work from within mainstream political
parties to effect change.

By the 1980s, French feminism seemed to have lost its momentum.[5]
Autonomous groups existed who campaigned around single issues, such
as rape and domestic violence, but the decade was generally perceived as
one of consolidation of previous gains. The establishment of a fully
fledged Ministry of Women's Rights following the election of François
Mitterrand as President in 1981 heralded a change in direction for French
feminism and the institutionalization of the feminist struggle. Headed by
Yvette Roudy, the Ministry claimed major victories, such as the 1983 Loi

---

[4] There is abundant material on the 1970s and early 1980s on developments in the French feminist
movement. One of the best studies remains Claire Duchen's *Feminism in France: From May '68 to
Mitterrand* (London: Routledge & Kegan Paul, 1986).

[5] For an overview of developments in French feminism over the 1980s and 1990s, see Gill Allwood
and Khursheed Wadia, 'French Feminism: National and International Perspectives', *Modern and
Contemporary France*, 10/2 (2002), 211–23.

Roudy on equality at work, but also defeats such as the 1983 Anti-Sexism bill. In 1986, with the election of a conservative administration, the Ministry disappeared, its activities absorbed into other departments.

In the 1990s, there has been a resurgence of feminist activities around reproduction rights, employment, and issues of equality between men and women. One of the most successful campaigns of the decade to mobilize both women and men was the campaign for parity or numerical equality for men and women in elected office.[6] By 1993, after nearly fifty years of political representation, a mere 6 per cent of deputies in the National Assembly were women, a rise of 0.3 per cent from the first legislative elections in 1945 where women were eligible to vote and stand as candidates. Calls for initiatives to increase women's participation in the political arena were heard in the early 1980s, such as feminist lawyer Gisèle Halimi's proposal to introduce quotas for women candidates in municipal elections. Such calls were in vain. By the early 1990s, however, the political landscape had changed. A co-ordinated campaign for parity succeeded in uniting a wide spectrum of political actors, all in agreement that reforming the founding Constitution of the Fifth French Republic would be the most effective means of ensuring progress.

In June 1999, legislation was passed amending articles 3 and 4 of the Constitution to read that 'the law favours the equal access of men and women to political office' and making it incumbent on political parties 'to contribute to the implementation of parity'. Those who opposed the legislation claimed that it was a regressive move that threatened the universalist principles of the French Republic whereby every citizen is eligible for office regardless of distinction. Although they recognized the importance of increasing women's participation in public life, they believed that mechanisms other than constitutional reform should be developed to achieve this aim. Those who supported the legislation argued that the 'evolutionary' approach to changing the gender profile of the National Assembly had patently failed over the post-war period and that half of humanity, so abysmally underrepresented, deserved better. They pointed to the highly masculinist culture of French political parties and institutions and to the fact that many male politicians were unwilling, even resistant, to reform. As France entered the twenty-first century, the time seemed ripe to 'féminiser la République' (feminize the Republic).

French women's writing of the 1990s has reflected the diverse interests and situations of French and Francophone women in social, political, and

[6] See Gill Allwood and Khursheed Wadia, *Women and Politics in France 1958–2000* (London: Routledge, 2000) for chapters examining the context, events, and debates of the parity campaign.

personal terms. As Gill Rye has discussed, women's writing of the decade
built upon the feminist debates of the 1970s and 1980s and produced a
rich set of writing practices reworking established narrative styles and
structures.[7] Rye points to the predominance of themes relating to identity
and selfhood, above all familial relationships and loss. However, in Rye's
survey of 1990s writing by French women, and in critical studies more
generally, there is a dearth of material on popular culture and women's
incursions into traditionally male-dominated genres, such as crime
fiction. This omission deserves to be corrected as the 1990s were an unprecedented decade for the emergence of a generation of French women
crime writers. Their rewriting of the generic conventions of the *roman
noir* was a revelation and attracted much critical attention. It seemed that
at last parity was on its way to transforming one of the last male bastions
of the French literary world: the *roman noir*.

French women writers and crime fiction

In the mid-1990s, a group of French women writers took the crime fiction
establishment by storm. Festivals and reviews gave prominence to
French women writers, such as Brigitte Aubert, Andrea H. Japp, Dominique Manotti, Maud Tabachnik, Sylvie Granotier, and Fred Vargas, and
predicted the advent of a new and exciting *polar au féminin* (feminine
crime fiction).[8] Media coverage implied that this sudden burst of activity
by French women crime writers was a new phenomenon. Indeed, reading
critical histories of the French *roman noir*, the reader could be forgiven for
thinking that French women writers have played little or no part in the
development of French detective and crime fiction over the twentieth
century.[9] Yet this would be a gross misrepresentation. It is not that French
women have rejected the genre. Rather, they have been systematically
written out of the history of French crime fiction, and more specifically
the *roman noir*. Whilst contemporary writers may have triggered renewed
interest in the contribution of women, many, including Maud Tabachnik,

[7]   Gill Rye, 'Women's Writing', in *Women in Contemporary France*, 133–51.
[8]   For an examination of this group of French women writers and media responses to their work, see
Véronique Desnain, '"La Femelle de l'espèce": Women in Contemporary French Crime Fiction',
French Cultural Studies, 12/2 (2001), 175–92.
[9]   In Jean-Pierre Schweighaeuser's *Le Roman noir français* (Paris: PUF, 1984), only one woman writer is
discussed, Janine Oriano. Even in more recent articles, such as Robert Deleuse's 'Petite histoire du
roman noir français', *Les Temps modernes*, 595 (1997), 53–87, only one woman is mentioned, Fred
Vargas, and even then the acknowledgement is grudging.

are aware that they write in the wake of a 'missing' tradition of French women's crime writing.[10]

French women writers have contributed to the corpus of French detective fiction from its inception. Research undertaken by Deborah Hamilton has uncovered over 180 French women writers publishing over 1,750 novels from the 1920s to the 1990s in France.[11] Yet the question remains why has their work been largely overlooked by critics and other writers? A number of factors come into play. First, Hamilton and others point to the difficulty of establishing the identity of women writers. A large percentage have published under male pseudonyms (as many as 40%). Hamilton's work shows up the prodigious output of some women writers hidden behind male pseudonyms, such as Claude Asnain (Halette Fernand-Gregh) who published over eighty titles in the 1940s and 1950s or Mario Ropp (Marie-Anne Devillier) who has published over a hundred titles in the famous Fleuve noir collection in recent years. Even today, some women writers choose masculine or androgynous pseudonyms, such as Fred Vargas, or use initials, or only a surname, implying a masculine identity. This strategy of gender disguise, whether willingly accepted or imposed by publishers, was reinforced in the early days of the *roman noir* when, in common with their male counterparts, French women writers used Anglo-American sounding pseudonyms, such as Mike Cooper (Liliane M. Gatineau). Doubly marginalized by gender and nationality, it was highly unlikely that any but a token few of the early women crime writers would be given credit for their work.

A second factor impeding recognition of women's contribution to the genre is the male-dominated culture of the detective and crime fiction publishing world. Certain collections, particularly the Série noire, have been perceived as aggressively macho and closed to women writers. The first women to be published in the series was an American, Gertrude Walker, in 1950 with *A contre-voie*, but readers had to wait until 1971 for the first novel by a French woman, *B comme Baptiste* by J(anine) Oriano. Another twelve years elapsed before a second French woman writer was published and then as one half of the writing duo, Marie et Joseph. In interview, Patrick Raynal, current editor of the Série noire, acknowledges the poor gender profile of the collection but attributes the lack of women writers to their reticence to adopt the style and perspective of the *roman noir*.[12] Under his influence, the collection has opened up to young French

---

[10] See Tabachnik, 'Remarques sur la non-place des femmes dans le roman noir', 123.

[11] The source of much material on the history of French women's crime fiction is Deborah Hamilton's 'The French Detective Novel 1920s–1990s: Gendering a Genre', Ph.D. thesis (Pennsylvania State University, 1994).   [12] Interview with Patrick Raynal, Paris, 13 February 2002.

women writers, such as Sylvie Granotier, Pascale Fonteneau, and Alix de Saint-André, but women's writing still remains a tiny percentage of the overall production, even taking into account the public appetite for American and British translations.[13] One explanation for the upsurge in French women's crime writing in the 1990s could be the arrival of women into senior positions in the publishing world. One good example is Viviane Hamy, founder of the *noir* Chemins nocturnes series, where seven of the current ten authors published are women.[14]

A third factor that has operated against women is age-old cultural assumptions about women's relationship to violence and criminality. Literary scholars of past and present persist in viewing women writers as better suited to traditional mystery novels or psychological thrillers with their understated depictions of sex and violence. Recently, critics have debated whether women writers' prominence as mystery novelists is partly compensation for failed personal lives, equating life with fiction,[15] or if 'the universe of the *polar* is intrinsically inimical to women'.[16] Whilst essentialist views over gender and genre are scarcely credible, a case can be made for deep-rooted socio-cultural factors affecting women's visibility in forms such as the *roman noir*. From its origins in the immediate post-war period, the French *roman noir* was marketed as a populist genre appealing to working-class male readers who felt some affinity with the struggles of the male protagonist battling against the combined forces of big business, the State, and the criminal underworld. By evacuating the contribution of women, the genre remained one that, as Deborah Hamilton comments, 'helped to reinforce a masculine subject identity for the *roman policier*'.[17] Narratives by and for men became the dominant model for the genre.

Reticence to acknowledge the contribution of women to the history of the *roman noir* or common assumptions about its innately 'masculine'

---

[13] In 1994, the number of women writers published in the Série noire was calculated at 4.3% of the total. Their national profile broke down as American (42), British (3), Australian (1), Swedish (1), and French (7), with five of the French authors first published during 1992–4. See *813*, 48 (October 1994).

[14] See Véronique Desnain, 'Le Polar féminin?: Contemporary Crime Writing by Women in France', http://www.selc.ed.ac/arachnofils/issue1/Desnain8.html. Desnain provides a useful overview of contemporary women's crime fiction, followed by valuable interviews with selected authors and editors.

[15] See Pierre Verdaguer discussing Dorothy L. Sayers in 'Considérations sur le roman policier féminin', in *La Séduction policière: signes de croissance d'un genre réputé mineur: Pierre Magnan, Daniel Pennac et quelques autres* (Birmingham, Ala.: Summa Publications, 1999), 144.

[16] Stephen Noreiko, '"Toutes des Salopes": Representation of Women in French Crime Fiction', *French Cultural Studies*, 10/1 (1999), 89–101 (90).

[17] Deborah Hamilton, 'The Roman Noir and the Reconstruction of National Identity in Postwar France', in Mullen and O'Beirne (eds), *Crime Scenes*, 228–40 (240).

ethos is not confined to France. Anglo-American feminist critics of crime
and detective fiction have taken great interest in the *roman noir*, discussing its potential as a radical form able to promote feminist reading
positions. Some are highly sceptical about its use, pointing to the common tropes and themes of such fiction. With its focus on the lone male
investigator, graphic depictions of violence, and conservative and sometimes reactionary attitudes towards gender roles, it seems to have little to
offer women writers and their concerns.[18] For such critics, the representation of women in the genre is at best stereotypical and at worst misogynist.
The figure of the *femme fatale*, as she appears in some of the great *roman
noir* classics such as Chandler's *The Big Sleep* (1939) or Hammett's *The
Maltese Falcon* (1929), is the archetypal sexual predator and betrayer of
the hero. Her sexuality is a weapon to seduce and disorientate the detective and her deadly beauty leads to the perdition of the more gullible male
characters.

Although a number of feminist critics doubt that such a form and its
main characters can be recuperated for feminist perspectives, others,
such as Priscilla L. Walton and Manina Jones, are more optimistic.[19] They
argue that popular genres are not stable and fixed and can be co-opted for
feminist purposes. For them, 'resistant' readings and rewritings are possible that transform generic rules and conventions and allow both women
readers and writers to refashion the world vision of male-dominated genres, such as hard-boiled detective fiction. One important strategy in this
process is the use of a reverse discourse 'that repeats and inverts the ideological imperative of the dominant discourse in order to authorize those
marginalized by it'.[20] In other words, women writers can subvert and rad-
icalize the rules of the *roman noir*, giving voice to perspectives, such as
those of women, ethnic minorities, and lesbian and gay characters, who
have traditionally been silenced by it. Walton and Jones focus particularly
on the American feminist crime writers of the 1980s, such as Sara Paretsky
and Sue Grafton. With their empowering and feisty women private eyes
and detectives, such writers spoke to a generation of women readers eager
for role models that no longer demeaned and trivialized women but
engaged in debates over female agency and power in the contemporary

[18] See Rosalind Coward and Linda Semple, 'Tracking Down the Past: Women and Detective Fiction', in
Helen Carr (ed.), *From My Guy to Sci-Fi: Genre and Women's Writing in the Postmodern World* (London:
Pandora, 1989), 39–57 (47).
[19] See Priscilla L. Walton and Manina Jones, *Detective Agency: Women Writing the Hard-Boiled Tradition*
(Berkeley: University of California Press, 1999).
[20] Walton and Jones, 'Does She Or Doesn't She?: The Problematics of Feminist Detection', in Maurizio
Ascari (ed.), *Two Centuries of Detective Fiction: A New Comparative Approach* (Bologna: University of
Bologna, 2000), 233–59 (238).

world.[21] Yet, Walton and Jones also recognize that, in placing women at the centre of the narrative, feminist crime fiction also reconfigures the gender norms of *noir* fiction. During the 1980s and 1990s, Anglo-American feminist crime fiction addressed important social issues, such as women's relationship to crime and the urban space, the gender bias of the justice system and the police, and attitudes towards domestic abuse, rape, and sexual violence. Spreading the net more widely than the resolution of a bloody murder, such texts interrogated women's position in society with highly politicized aims and posited crime as 'the logical outgrowth of an order built on the oppression of women'.[22]

French women crime writers to the 1990s have, in some cases, taken on board the challenge of reworking the *roman noir* with gender as a key feature. Not all crime fiction written by women is feminist in intention and it would be misleading to believe that debates around gender inflect the work of every woman writer.[23] Of those French women writers who engage critically with male crime fiction traditions, few would openly label their work as feminist. Indeed, those who are prepared to accept that they have a different relationship to the *roman noir* because of their gender refute the idea of a school or particular movement of French women's crime writing, believing this to be yet another way of ghettoizing women writers.[24] Yet, as Véronique Desnain has demonstrated in her work on contemporary French women crime writers, similarities in theme and preoccupation can be detected. The group of women crime fiction writers who first gained prominence in the mid-1990s tend to focus on victims of crime, such as women and children, and the long-term consequences of abuse and violence. Like their American counterparts, such writers pay close attention to the private sphere and personal relationships and there is a marked preference for choosing narrating figures who stand on the periphery of society, such as the homeless or the physical and mentally handicapped.[25] Maud Tabachnik's *Un été pourri* represents one of the more overtly feminist texts in this corpus of writing from the 1990s. With its story of serial killers on the loose in Boston one hot summer, it provides

---

[21] Not so for Sally Munt in *Murder by the Book: Feminism and the Crime Novel* (London: Routledge, 1994) who is particularly scathing about liberal feminist crime fiction 'functioning within a fantasy environ of post-feminist opportunity' (31).

[22] Quoted in Sandra Tonc, 'Questing Women: The Feminist Mystery After Feminism', in Glenwood Irons (ed.), *Feminism in Women's Detective Fiction* (London: University of Toronto Press, 1995), 46–63 (47).

[23] For example, see the close textual reading of Fred Vargas's novels in Sara Poole, '*Rompols* not of the Bailey: Fred Vargas and the *polar* as *mini-proto-mythe*', *French Cultural Studies*, 12/1 (2001), 95–108. Poole's analysis is focused exclusively on the linguistic play and wit of Vargas's novels.

[24] See the comments of Dominique Manotti quoted in Desnain, 'La Femelle de l'espèce', 178–9.

[25] See Sylvie Granotier, *Dodu* (2000) and Brigitte Aubert, *La Mort des bois* (1996) respectively.

a sustained reflection on sexual violence against women, gender relations in contemporary society, and the threat that masculine power and privilege pose to the social order.

Maud Tabachnik and the feminist thriller

Tabachnik's first novel, *La vie à fleur de terre*, was published in 1990 but it was her second novel, *Un été pourri* (1994), that was to act as her major breakthrough into the crime fiction world. Published in the newly created Chemins nocturnes series under the editorship of Viviane Hamy, the text excited much debate and commentary for its depiction of women as the perpetrators of extreme violence against men. In her article for *Les Temps modernes* on women's crime fiction, Tabachnik writes of the threatening phone messages left on her answering machine by enraged male readers and the questions of journalists who asked her if she had something against men to make them the victims of such gruesome sexual mutilation and murder.[26] As Tabachnik notes with some irony, these journalists were operating sexual double standards, for it seemed that few of them were prepared to challenge the motives of writers, such as James Ellroy, who depicted dismembered female bodies in far more graphic detail.

After the success (and notoriety) of *Un été pourri*, Tabachnik went on to create a series of novels featuring one or both of the main protagonists from the novel, Sandra Kahn, a lesbian investigative journalist, and Sam Goodman, the conscience-stricken police detective. Tabachnik has not confined herself to these characters nor to the setting of contemporary America. She has also written historical detective novels, such as *L'Étoile du temple* (1997) set in France during the Middle Ages, as well as thrillers of historical memory in the mode of Didier Daeninckx, such as *La Mémoire du bourreau* (1999) which deals with the legacy of Nazi war criminals. Yet even with these changes in location, time, and character, her work is always articulated in feminist terms.

In her article for *Les Temps modernes*, 'Remarques sur la non-place des femmes dans le roman noir', Tabachnik deplores the clichés and stereotypes of a genre that has traditionally relegated women to the roles of dutiful wife, secretary, mother substitute, victim, and *femme fatale*. Whilst she recognizes that French women writers are a decade behind their American counterparts in producing credible female alternatives to these

---

[26] Tabachnik, 'Remarques sur la non-place des femmes dans le roman noir', 125–6.

two-dimensional models, she is aware that the 'superwomen' of such narratives are not necessarily the most appropriate vehicle for countering the misogynist tendencies of the *roman noir*. Her own response to such images is not to produce substitute heroines but rather to focus on victims, particularly women as victims of sexual violence. *Un été pourri* illustrates this with its depiction of women who fight back. The 'reverse discourse' highlighted by Walton and Jones operates here in the reworking of images of women as passive victims of violence. Instead, in *Un été pourri*, female protagonists take revenge on the men who have raped and abused either the women themselves or ones that they have loved. They outwit the police, circumvent the justice system, and overturn perceptions of women as fearful and timorous creatures. As Tabachnik herself commented, she planned to show how a woman 'est capable de se battre, de défendre la société, de ne pas vivre dans la peur, de ne pas seulement subir de violences mais de les rendre, de se débrouiller sans l'assistance d'un homme'.[27] It is this avowed subversion of sexual stereotypes that disturbed so many readers and critics.

Un été pourri: 'de l'autre coté du miroir'[28]

Un été pourri is set in Boston one torrid summer as a serial murder investigation unfolds. Four men are found with their throats slit and their penises and/or testicles cut off and placed either beside them or in their pockets. Different weapons are used for three of the murders and the second two seem to be carried out by left-handed killers. One of the policemen in charge of the investigation is Sam Goodman, an elegant and well-dressed senior officer, who, for much of the narrative, follows up traditional sources looking to locate the lone (male) psychopath who fits the police profile for such sexually motivated killings. No clues are unearthed and when a drug addict eventually 'confesses' to the murders after a brutal police interrogation, Goodman instinctively understands that the whole department had become blinkered in its pursuit of a single male killer. However, he, like many other male characters in the text, refuses to confront what seems inconceivable: that the killer or killers could be women:

---

[27] 'is capable of fighting, defending society, not living in fear, not submitting to violence but inflicting it, managing without the help of a man'. Ibid. 129.
[28] 'on the other side of the mirror'. Maud Tabachnik, *Un été pourri* (Paris: Éditions Viviane Hamy, 1994), 182.

'Les femmes ne tuent pas de la même facon que les hommes [. . .] Une femme n'a pas la pulsion criminelle aussi violente qu'un homme. Le crime d'une femme est la plupart du temps prémédité. Elle va rarement tuer dans un geste de colère, ou alors pour défendre les siens.'
   'Qui vous dit qu'il n'y pas une femme qui prémédite de supprimer les types à la vie sexuelle un peu agitée?'
   Sam secoua la tête.[29]

The journalist Thomas Herman, a close friend of Sam's, has unwittingly uncovered the main motivation for the series of killings. As the novel progresses, the reader is drawn increasingly to conclude that the four killings have been committed by four different people (three women and a man) who have targeted men associated with violent and/or deviant sexual behaviour: from rape and murder to domestic violence and propositioning strangers. Goodman's traditionalist views of women as the weaker sex mean that he is unable to comprehend that there is sexual equality in all things, even murder.

   Throughout the text, Tabachnik challenges a vision of women as the passive sex who bear suffering in silence. Although the killings are not co-ordinated and the killers themselves do not communicate with one another, there are commonalities that link their actions. The first murder of Mort Newman by Fanny Mitchell is complicated by the reader's discovery that Fanny, along with her mother, was raped by her drunken stepfather and his friend. This assault led to her mother being interned in a nursing home and Fanny spending the rest of her adolescence passed between different children's homes. The long-term effects of such sexual violence on Fanny are an obsessive concern with cleanliness, an eating disorder, and a complete inability to form sexual relationships with men. In the case of the second murder of Freddy Latimer, the killer is revealed to be Sandra Khan who avenges the rape and murder of her lover, Joan Shimutz, killed exactly one year earlier. Joan's murder was never officially solved by the police for lack of evidence. Freddy Latimer's continued threat to society is further emphasized in the text as, when he first appears to the reader, he is escaping yet another charge for rape, this time of the young Carmen Sanchez, 10 years old and unable to recover from the trauma of the attack.

   These two women's subsequent killings are presented, therefore, as a justified response to extreme sexual violence. Fanny is attacked by the

[29] 'Women don't kill in the same way as men [...] A woman's criminal urges are not as violent as a man's. Crimes by women are mostly premeditated. A woman rarely kills in anger or then only to defend her own./ Who says that there isn't a woman who plans to do away with guys with rather troubled sex lives?/ Sam shook his head.' Tabachnik, *Un été pourri*, 173.

drunken council worker Mort Newman and kills in self-defence. Sandra takes revenge on Joan's killer. In both cases, extreme sexual violence is part of a revenge fantasy where the violence perpetrated against women and children has been revisited on the men themselves. By providing such compelling cases for women as 'victimes agissantes',[30] women who fight back, Tabachnik asks the reader to consider if in fact the male victims are not more guilty than their female murderers and whether these women are not merely responding to sexual violence that regularly goes unpunished, such as domestic violence. Tabachnik makes it clear that, but for Sandra Khan's murder of Latimer, he would have benefited from judicial complacency and indifference and moved away from Boston to carry on committing more atrocious crimes against women. Indeed, the novel challenges the conventional views of policemen such as Sam Goodman, that women killers are an unnatural phenomenon. In the narrative, they are presented as developing precisely in response to patriarchal society's treatment of them as sexual objects.

Un été pourri presents such extreme sexual violence as an extension of fraught and unhappy relations between men and women in general. Sam Goodman is struck by how many of the women he meets consider the killings to be a justified 'exécution' (execution).[31] Even his Jewish mother and her circle of friends feel a sense of morbid satisfaction, seeing it as men's turn to experience fear and anxiety on the streets at night: 'C'est bien fait pour leurs pieds! tonna la mère de Sam dans un mouvement énergique du menton. C'est toujours les femmes jusqu'ici qui se faisaient assassiner par des fous.'[32] Sam imagines the possibility that for the women of Boston, these killings give them a secret pleasure: 'une espèce de revanche sur la vie, sur le sadisme des hommes, sur leur brutalité'.[33]

This bleak image of gender relations is contextualized in the book by presenting a series of dysfunctional and failing sexual relationships. Marriage is presented as either a source of abuse and violence, as with Fanny's stepfather and mother, or as a sham, as in the case of Augusta and Ron Magnusson, the couple whom friends envy for their compatibility and apparent marital bliss. Both successful in different professional arenas, Augusta as a respected lawyer and Ron as a university professor, their public image belies personal pain and tragedy. Augusta is repulsed

---

[30] This concept is developed across a range of contemporary French women's crime fiction in Desnain, 'La Femelle de l'espèce', 186–90.   [31] Tabachnik, *Un été pourri*, 61, 79.

[32] '"That will teach them a thing or two!" thundered Sam's mother vigorously nodding her head. "Until now, it has always been women who have got themselves murdered by mad men."' Tabachnik, *Un été pourri*, 158.

[33] 'A kind of revenge on life, on men's sadism, on their brutality.' Tabachnik, *Un été pourri*, 206.

by her sexual desires, reinforced by her strict religious education, and berates herself as a nymphomaniac and sexual obsessive. After a riding accident, Ron becomes impotent, even though doctors tell him that this is a psychological rather than physical condition. The depths of Augusta's self-loathing are revealed in her adulterous relationship with Sam Goodman whom she treats as a mere sexual object in a striking gender role reversal.[34] Sam is left as the unhappy and damaged lover who waits for phone calls and remains unable to comprehend the actions of the woman he loves.

There seems no possibility of a sexual relationship between men and women that is not predicated to some degree on emotional or physical abuse. Even the sympathetic character of Thomas Herman, besotted with Fanny Mitchell, is capable of forcing drunken advances on his girlfriend that end their burgeoning relationship. The logical conclusion of such miscommunication and simmering violence is the complete breakdown of any form of heterosexual relationship. Fanny Mitchell epitomizes this as she descends into madness in the last chapters of the book. She ends by seeing all men as bestial creatures who should be hunted down and killed after the treatment women have suffered at their hands: 'Quand donc le comprendraient-elles? Combien leur fallait-il de viols, d'abandons, d'incestes, de coups pour qu'elles décident à passer à l'attaque. Elles devraient les terroriser comme elles l'avaient été depuis la nuit des temps.'[35]

The only optimistic portrayal of sexual relations comes from the lesbian figure of Sandra Kahn whose love of Joan Schmitz leads her to avenge her death by killing Latimer. She is the only character by the end of the novel to have formed a mutually fulfilling sexual and emotional relationship with the university professor, Nina Garcia-Marquez, and she is surrounded by friends, such as Thomas Herman, who are prepared to organize her defence when Sam discovers her identity as the second murderer. Reader identification with the lesbian figure is further enhanced by the narrative strategies of the text. She is the only character presented to the reader in the first person so that insight is gained into her motivations and actions. In early sections of the book, the reader is unsure who this first-person narrator is, other than a premeditated killer. However, this characterization changes over the course of the novel and textual clues as

[34] Sam becomes her 'étalon' (stallion) whom she claims to see for purely sexual pleasure and with little or no emotional involvement (225).
[35] 'When then would they realize? How many cases of rape, desertion, incest and violence would it take for women to decide to take action? They should terrorize men like men had terrorized them since the dawn of time.' Tabachnik, *Un été pourri*, 251.

to her profession, religious background, and sexual preferences eventually link the second killer to the figure of Sandra Khan. As she is presented in other chapters from a third-person viewpoint as a vivacious and likable character, the reader comes to adopt Goodman's sympathetic perspective on her actions, an attitude that eventually leads him to pull back from indicting her for murder. Yet if it seems that lesbian relationships offer the one possibility of genuine happiness in the novel this is not to be attributed solely to the brutality of individual men. Tabachnik also explores how men are the victims of a patriarchal social order that threatens the emotional and physical wellbeing of all.

Un été pourri presents the reader with starkly contrasting images of masculinity. On the one hand, the reader is faced with characters who represent the violence, ignorance, and misogyny of Western culture: rapists and murderers such as Mort Newman and Freddy Latimer and sexual predators such as Rodney Stockton who accosts strangers on the metro. On the other hand, the novel shows the reader angst-ridden men in crisis, such as Sam Goodman and Thomas Herman, whose feminine traits lead them to sympathize with the damaged women with whom they come into contact.[36] Both have relationships with murderers, Sam with Augusta and Thomas with Fanny. They end up hurt and bewildered by these women, genuinely unable to understand their behaviour: 'Il [Sam] réalisa tout à coup combien les femmes, en partant de la première qu'il avait connue et qui lui avait donné le jour, lui étaient totalement étrangères.'[37]

In Sam's case, these feminine traits run counter to the machismo of the police force. Not one woman is presented as involved in the murder investigation and aggressive male rivalry and infighting impede police work as men jockey for power and prestige in the race to corner the killers. This is heightened by the pressure exerted by the (male) mayor who fears the effects of the killings on the forthcoming elections. Sam's refusal to stomach the intimidation of witnesses and his clear empathy for the killers leave him on the margins of an institution that is presented as very little interested in crimes against women (the killing and sexual mutilation of two women the previous summer goes unsolved) and pools all its resources once men are the prime targets. As the first-person narration of Sandra Kahn makes clear early in the text, once Joan's murder has become the investigation of a lesbian, the only real question that interests the

---

[36] Goodman and Herman are, just as their names suppose, on the side of the angels with feminized character traits. Mort Newman is a parody of the 'New Man' and his only contribution to the text is as the dead man ('mort'), emasculated by the women killers.

[37] 'He [Sam] realized suddenly the extent to which women were totally foreign to him, starting with the first he had know and who had given him life.' Tabachnik, *Un été pourri*, 204.

policemen in charge is 'pourquoi deux belles filles comme nous restaient entre elles'.[38]

At the extreme end of this spectrum of damaged men is Ron Magnusson, Augusta's husband, an emasculated man whose impotence leads him to kill an exhibitionist who deliberately arouses him on a crowded metro train. Ron's violent response to his attraction and repulsion for such an individual shows how far the façade of marital happiness hides misery and depression. Prepared to countenance Augusta's affair with Sam, his emulation of the women killers illustrates his ambivalence towards men and his own masculinity as he cuts off the penis, primary symbol of male prowess. Yet, by the end of the book, this act has not led to Ron's psychological downfall. Rather it has acted as a release as he and Augusta are represented in the last chapter preparing for a tennis game with influential friends. They seem closer than ever. What is the reader to make of an ending in which three of the four killers have escaped the law? Sandra, Augusta, and Ron seem destined to live happily ever after and are untroubled by guilt or shame.

Reader responses

With its open ending, *Un été pourri* challenges the reader to consider if the murdered men deserved their violent deaths and if their killings were comprehensible, even justified, in the light of the killers' life experiences. Fanny's guilt is proved when police discover the razor used for the killing of Mort Newman at her workplace but her unstable mental state will be used to attenuate her actions. It is significant that Sam Goodman, the character whose perspective colours our perception of the investigation, eventually drops the case, although he discovers the identity of two of the killers, Fanny and Sandra. Talking to his friend Thomas Herman, Sam compares himself to a hunter who has cornered his prey but feels ill equipped to go in for the kill: 'Imaginez un chasseur qui se serait crevé à pister son gibier et qui au moment de l'abattre s'aperçoit qu'il a oublié ses cartouches ou que le calibre ne correspond pas à son fusil. Eh, bien, j'en suis là.'[39] Sam understands the women's motivations and possibly endorses their actions. Yet these feelings are in contradiction with his

---

[38] 'why two pretty girls like us were a couple'. Tabachnik, *Un été pourri*, 75.

[39] 'Imagine a hunter who has worn himself out tracking down his prey and, just as he goes in for the kill, discovers that he has forgotten his gun cartridges or that the calibre doesn't match his rifle. Well, that's how I feel.' Tabachnik, *Un été pourri*, 268.

professional duties as a police officer to track down offenders and arrest the main culprits. By the end of the novel, Sam accepts a posting to New York, fudging his personal and professional allegiances. Where does this leave the reader? Do we too experience an inner struggle, sympathizing with the killers but wanting their arrest? The strategies of the text work against any clear-cut resolution.

First, the reader is not privy to the gruesome scenes of killing and mutilation. The only details of the killings come from bald police statements and the descriptions of the murder scenes do not linger on physical details. Such descriptions are primarily focused on the deviant behaviour of the victims immediately prior to their deaths. With little graphic description of the deaths, we are not encouraged to focus on the brutality of the killers. Secondly, we do not view the female and male perpetrators as psychopathic killers. Apart from Fanny, who descends into madness, these are not characters who represent a threat to society. In fact, they are all respectable and hard-working members of the community, the women, ironically, all involved to some degree with the workings of the judiciary or the police.[40] They are presented as vigilante figures, characters who fight back, and who, in at least three of the murders, have punished individuals who represent some kind of sexual threat to others. The case of Jimmy di Maggio, the third victim, is the most ambivalent of the four, killed after a tussle with his girlfriend in a park late at night and not assumed to be a sexual predator like the others. Here the killing seems the least defensible of all but the doubts it raises are not pursued in the book. Lastly, the text blurs the lines between victim and perpetrator in ways that vindicate the killings. Those who commit the crimes are portrayed as innocent victims of other sex crimes or victims of repressive social taboos and conventions, such as Augusta. By the book's close, we are inclined to feel satisfied that justice has not been done and that this is the best possible conclusion.

Un été pourri raises the question of gendered readings. Do male and female readers have different responses to the serial killings of men? In a straw poll of students who studied the text, it seemed difficult to establish the existence of what Kathleen Klein has called a 'double-voiced discourse' where gender is the defining factor in interpreting the text.[41] Unease was felt by all students about the sexual mutilations but the vision of dissected bodies on show in contemporary Anglo-American crime

---

[40] Augusta is a criminal lawyer, Fanny an assistant to the District Attorney, and Sandra an investigative journalist who works on crime stories. Their double lives as upholders and breakers of the law makes their capture that much more difficult for Sam Goodman.

[41] Cited in Walton and Jones, 'Does She Or Doesn't She?: The Problematics of Feminist Detection', 237.

fiction and film lessens the taboo of Tabachnik's revisionist imagery. This acceptance of women writers and their rewriting of *roman noir* conventions can be attributed to a changing social and political climate. Women writers can now tell a different tale from the clichés of previous generations. French women writers today, such as Tabachnik, are challenging prevalent views of gender and genre and showing the 'other side of the mirror'; how women characters need not be reduced to fear and victimization but can adopt different subject positions. New possibilities are opening up for sexuality, ethnicity, and gender to be addressed in the *roman noir*. Indeed, such traditionally marginalized issues promise to reinvent tired and formulaic fictions. With a swathe of French women writers poised to shake up the French *roman noir*, exciting new work may yet 'féminiser le polar' in unexpected ways and to the benefit of all.

Conclusion

mais ce roman est bien plus qu'un polar.[1]

In April 2002, the prestigious literary journal the *Nouvelle Revue française* devoted a section to 'l'avenir de la fiction' (the future of fiction). The editor Michel Brandeau chose to present the series of commissioned articles as an investigation into the crisis facing the contemporary French novel. In his introductory comments, he dubs his contributors well-qualified 'detectives', able to diagnose the problem and suggest possible futures for a literary establishment in dire need of renewal. From the opening lines of the section, it is clear, therefore, that paradigms of detective fiction are to play an important part in the discussion.

Benjamin Berton is one of several young contributors who set out to survey trends in the modern French novel. His article provides a trenchant critique of contemporary writing in France as he reproaches French novelists with an 'engagement modéré dans l'époque' and 'un tel manque d'agression et de lucidité sociale'.[2] In this, they lag way behind their British and American counterparts. For Berton, the French novelistic tradition of the twenty-first century is either reliant on old schools and models of literature or given over to titillating autobiographical revelations. In the former category, Berton focuses on the bourgeois novel of manners and the psychological introspection of recent novels by writers such as Marie Darrieussecq and Christophe Donner, while the clear target of the second category is the exhibitionist prose of Catherine Millet's *La Vie sexuelle de Catherine M.*, one of the most talked about books of 2001.

In contrast to these traditions, Berton praises a rather eclectic group of writers that he classifies as 'réalistes modernes' (modern realists) and whom he sees as appropriating literary forms as a means of commenting

---

[1] 'but this novel is a lot more than crime fiction'. Jean-Patrick Manchette quoted in Patrick Raynal, 'Et si nous parlions un peu de l'avenir du roman noir?', *Nouvelle Revue française*, 561 (April 2002), 169–76 (174). Manchette was ridiculing the sentiment of critics who seemed unable to credit the *polar* and *roman noir* with any literary worth.

[2] 'a moderate commitment to the era', and 'such a lack of aggression and social lucidity'. Benjamin Berton, 'Des plans sur la comète: panorama prospectif du roman français moderne', *Nouvelle Revue française*, 561, 160–8 (161).

on their times. The novels of Maurice G. Dantec and Michel Houellebecq are deliberately disturbing with their focus on dark and dystopian futures for the human condition; neuroscience and crime fiction in Dantec's *Les Racines du Mal* (1995) and genetic revolution and the end of humanity in Houellebecq's *Les Particules élémentaires* (1999). For Berton, such authors have opened up the novel to new influences and narrative possibilities, drawing on popular genres such as science fiction, the adventure story, and detective fiction. They dialogue with other media and forms of communication. They create political and often insurrectionary visions of the future, anticipating social change. They are, in a word, *noir* novelists and, for Berton, they bring together many of the ingredients that will make up the future French literary *chef d'œuvre*.

Other contributors echo this perception of the future of French fiction. For Michel Le Bris, the resurgence of interest in the *roman noir* is connected to the contemporary geo-political situation. After 11 September 2001, Western civilization has entered a different phase. The spectre of worldwide terrorism and its infiltration of what had seemed some of the most secure spaces in the Western world means that literature has to redefine its role and to engage more fully in the present. The question is 'quelle écriture de désastre trouver pour dire ces ténèbres de sang?'[3] Contemporary and hybrid forms of the *roman noir* are, for Le Bris, one way of relating to this reconfigured world order. With its roots in a different period of crisis, the economic and social deprivations of interwar America, the *roman noir* seems well suited to capture the zeitgeist of a generation and to respond to the anxieties and fears of our age. For Le Bris, *noir* is the future of fiction 'parce que le future devenu notre présent se révèle noir. Définitivement noir.'[4]

For contributors such as Berton and Le Bris, the *roman noir* represents the amalgam of form and content, aesthetics and ethics, that promises to renew French novelistic traditions. As writing from the margins, it operates with a counter-cultural perspective that makes it an invaluable tool for challenging the status quo and contesting the values and ideals of its readers. The vocation of the contemporary *roman noir* is both to offer new narrative possibilities to young novelists and to act as 'littérature contestataire' (literature of contestation), a politicized means of expression that draws on present-day concerns and mediates the crises of the age. Yet, lurking behind such plaudits for *noir* writing is a pervasive sense of unease about the place of French literature in a globalized market. No longer able

---

[3] 'Which writing of disaster can be found to speak of this bloody darkness?' Michel Le Bris, 'Du nouveau, le roman noir', *Nouvelle Revue française*, 561, 141–58 (142).

[4] 'because the future that has become our present is shown to be noir. Conclusively noir'. Ibid. 153.

to rely on the cultural prestige of French as a language of international distinction, a number of the *Nouvelle Revue française* contributors betray their anxiety that France is fast losing out to Anglo-American competitors. *Noir* would seem not only to be the future of French fiction but one of its sole means of survival.

The current vogue for the *roman noir* has conferred belated recognition on over fifty years of French *noir* writing.[5] Yet, as it is hoped that this book has shown, the *roman noir* in French fiction and film has been fulfilling a social and political vocation that did not suddenly spring into being in the 1990s. Over the decades, French authors have shown their readiness to tackle some of most controversial issues of the day, such as decolonization and immigration, the legacy of the Second World War, and gender politics and equality. A sense of social and political commitment has played an integral part in the vision of individual authors and it is no coincidence that the majority of authors in this study write from a left-wing perspective. Few French authors of note could have been chosen who subscribe to right-wing views for it seems a mark of the French *roman noir* that *gauchiste* attitudes motivate and inform writers and their literary projects. What unites all the authors studied, however, is an urge to comment on the world around them, to dissect what is presented on our television screens and in our newspapers. Suspicion, doubt, and a healthy disregard for received views mean that the French *roman noir* remains a form of protest writing, ready to engage in a battle of words with a conservative and often reactionary social order.

In one sense then, the *polar* is more than a novel; it is a cultural narrative of our times. It is a literary form that sets out to cast a jaundiced eye over the past and present and to overturn our preconceptions and assumptions about the future. It contributes to the construction of our social and cultural identities and mediates change and turbulence in ways that encourage thought and reflection. The *roman noir* is, as David Platten suggests, a social history of our era and 'its legacy will be an unparalleled insight into the way we lived in the latter part of the twentieth century, to how we thought of ourselves, and to the nature of the society we have formed'.[6] This legacy is also intertwined with its history as a

---

[5] Patrick Raynal in 'Et si nous parlions un peu de l'avenir du roman noir?' makes the point that the late 1990s have witnessed the validation of the *roman noir* in many important intellectual outlets. He cites the special issue of *Les Temps modernes* in 1997 devoted to the *roman noir*, his own contribution to a volume of *Esprit* in February 1995, 'Le roman noir est l'avenir de la fiction', and the recent decision by the Pléiade collection to published a selection of Georges Simenon's detective fiction to mark the anniversary of his death.

[6] David Platten. 'Polar Positions: On the Theme of Identity in Contemporary *Noir* Fiction', *Nottingham French Studies*, 41/1 (Spring 2002), 5–18 (18).

literary form, as a genre that has proved highly adaptable over the years, able to respond to different historical, social, and political contexts. If the future of French fiction is in jeopardy, then, as Patrick Raynal, current editor of the Série noire, notes mischievously, the future of the *roman noir* seems secure: 'il n'a pas beaucoup de souci à se faire pour son avenir vu qu'il représente déjà une bonne moitié des œuvres romanesques dans le monde depuis qu'il existe'.[7] The future is bright for such dark fiction.

---

[7] 'There is little need to worry about its future considering that, since its introduction, it has represented a good half of the world's novelistic production.' Patrick Raynal, 'Et si nous parlions un peu de l'avenir du roman noir?', 175.

Select Bibliography

Alfu, *Léo Malet: parcours d'une œuvre* (Amiens: Encrage, 1998).

Allwood, Gill, and Khursheed Wadia, *Women and Politics in France 1958–2000* (London: Routledge, 2000).

—— 'French Feminism: National and International Perspectives', *Modern and Contemporary France*, 10/2 (2002), 211–23.

Amila, John, *Y a pas de bon dieu* (Paris: Gallimard, 1950).

—— *La Lune d'Omaha* (Paris: Gallimard, 1964).

Atack, Margaret, *May 68 in French Fiction and Film: Rethinking Society, Rethinking Representation* (Oxford: Oxford University Press, 1999).

Aubert, Brigitte, *La Mort des bois* (Paris: Éditions du Seuil, 1996).

Aveline, Claude, 'Le Roman policier est-il un genre littéraire?', *L'Œil du chat* (Paris: Mercure de France, 1970).

Baudrillard, Jean, *La Société de consommation: ses mythes et ses structures* (Paris: SGPP, 1970).

Benacquista, Tonino, *La Commedia des ratés* (Paris: Gallimard, 1991).

Blanc, Jean-Noël, *Polarville: images de la ville dans le roman policier* (Lyon: Presses Universitaires de Lyon, 1991).

Blatt, David, 'Immigrant Politics in a Republican Nation' in Alec Hargreaves and Mark McKinney (eds.), *Post-Colonial Cultures in France* (London: Routledge, 1997), 40–55.

Boileau, Pierre, and Thomas Narcejac, *Celle qui n'était plus/Les Diaboliques* (Paris: Denoël, 1952).

—— *D'entre les morts* (Paris: Denoël, 1954).

—— *Les Louves* (Paris: Denoël, 1955).

—— *Le Roman policier* (Paris: PUF, 1975).

—— 'Entretien', in *Cinématographique*, 63 (December 1980), 19–21.

Bond, David J., 'Daniel Pennac: des Histoires d'histoires', *LittéRéalité*, 10/2 (1998), 53–60.

Borde, Raymond, and Étienne Chaumeton, *Panorama du film noir américain* (Paris: Éditions de Minuit, 1955).

Bridgeman, Theresa, 'Paris-Polar in the Fog: Power of Place and Generic Space in Malet's *Brouillard au Pont Tolbiac*', *Australian Review of French Studies*, 35/1 (January–April 1998), 58–74 (62).

Buss, Robin, *French Film Noir* (London: Marion Boyars, 1994).

Callois, Roger, 'Puissances du roman', in *Approches de l'imaginaire* (Paris: Gallimard, 1974), 177–205.

Cawelti, John G., 'The Study of Literary Formulas', reproduced in Robin Winks (ed.), *Detective Fiction: A Collection of Critical Essays* (Englewood Cliffs, NJ: Prentice Hall, 1980), 121–43.

Chandler, Raymond, *The Big Sleep* (London: Hamish Hamilton, 1939).

—— 'The Simple Art of Murder', in *Pearls are a Nuisance* (Harmondsworth: Penguin Books, 1966), 181–99.

Conan, Eric, and Henry Rousso, *Vichy, un passé qui ne passe pas* (Paris: Fayard, 1994).

Conrath, Robert E., 'Pulp fixation: le roman noir américain et son lecteur français d'après-guerre', *La Révue génerale*, 12 (1995), 37–45.

Coward, Rosalind, and Linda Semple, 'Tracking Down the Past: Women and Detective Fiction', in Helen Carr (ed.), *From My Guy to Sci-Fi: Genre and Women's Writing in the Postmodern World* (London: Pandora, 1989), 39–57.

Daeninckx, Didier, *Meurtres pour mémoire* (Paris: Gallimard, 1984).

—— *Écrire en contre: Entretiens avec Robert Deleuse, Christine Cadet, Philippe Videlier* (Vénissieux: Éditions Paroles de l'Aube, 1997).

—— *Le Goût de la vérité* (Paris: Éditions Verdier, 1997).

Dantec, Maurice G., *Les Racines du Mal* (Paris: Gallimard, 1995).

Davis, Colin, and Elizabeth Fallaize, *French Fiction in the Mitterrand Years: Memory, Narrative, Desire* (Oxford: Oxford University Press, 2000).

Debord, Guy, *La Société de spectacle* (Paris: Éditions Champ Libre, 1971; repr. 1983).

Deloux, Jean-Pierre, 'Le Noir new-look', *Magazine littéraire*, 194 (April 1983), 21–3.

—— 'Grandeurs et servitudes policières . . .' *Polar*, 3 (1991), 9–24.

Desnain, Véronique, ' "La Femelle de l'espèce": Women in Contemporary French Crime Fiction', *French Cultural Studies*, 12/2 (2001), 175–92.

—— 'Le Polar féminin?: Contemporary Crime Writing by Women in France', www.selc.ed.ac/arachnofils/issue1/desnain8.html.

Duchen, Claire, *Feminism in France: From May '68 to Mitterrand* (London: Routledge & Kegan Paul, 1986).

Durozoi, Gérard, 'Esquisse pour un portrait anthume de Léo Malet en auteur de romans policiers', *Revue des sciences humaines*, 193 (January–March 1984), 169–78.

Forbes, Jill, *The Cinema in France: After the New Wave* (Basingstoke: Macmillan, 1992).

Forsdick, Charles, ' "Direction les oubliettes des l'histoire": Witnessing the Past in Contemporary French Polar', *French Cultural Studies*, 12/3 (October 2002), 333–50.

Gérault, Jean-François, *Jean-Patrick Manchette* (Amiens: Encrage, 2002).

Golsan, Richard J. (ed.), *Memory and Justice on Trial: The Papon Affair* (London: Routledge, 2000).

Granotier, Sylvie, *Dodu* (Paris: Gallimard, 2000).

Gregory, Abigail, and Ursula Tidd (eds.), *Women in Contemporary France* (Oxford: Berg, 2000).

Halling, Kirsten, and Roger Célestin, 'Interview with Daniel Pennac: The Writer's Trade, Detective Fiction, and Popular Culture', *Sites*, 1/1 (Spring 1997), 333–47.

Hamilton, Deborah, 'The French Detective Novel 1920s–1990s: Gendering a Genre', Ph.D. thesis (Pennsylvania State University, 1994).

Hammett, Dashiell, *The Maltese Falcon* (New York: Alfred A. Knopf, 1929).

Haywood, Susan, 'Simone Signoret (1921–1985)—The Body Political', *Women's Studies International Forum*, 23/6 (2000), 739–47.

Héléna, André, *Le Bon Dieu s'en fout* (Paris: Éditions New World Press, 1949).

Horsley, Lee, *The Noir Thriller* (Basingstoke: Palgrave, 2001).

Houellebecq, Michel, *Les Particules élémentaires* (Paris: Flammarion, 1999).

Jackson, Julian, *France: The Dark Years 1940–1944* (Oxford: Oxford University Press, 2001).

Japp, Andréa, *La Femelle de l'espèce* (Paris: Éditions du Masque-Hachette Livre, 1996).

Japrisot, Sébastien, *Un piège pour Cendrillon* (Paris: Denoël, 1962).

Jonquet, Thierry, *Mygale* (Paris: Gallimard, 1984).

—— *La Bête et la Belle* (Paris: Gallimard, 1985).

Kuisel, Richard, *Seducing the French: The Dilemma of Americanization* (Berkeley: University of California Press, 1993).

—— 'The Fernandel Factor: The Rivalry Between the French and American Cinema in the 1950s', *Yale French Studies*, 98 (2000), 119–34.

Lacassin, Francis, *Mythologie du roman policier* (Paris: UGE, 1974).

Lacombe, Alain, *Le Roman noir américain* (Paris: UGE, 1975).

Le Breton, Auguste, *Du rififi chez les hommes* (Paris: Gallimard, 1953).

Lebrun, Michel, and Jean-Pierre Schweighaeuser, *Le Guide du polar* (Paris: Syros, 1987).

Lhomeau, Franck, 'Les Débuts de la Série noire', *813*, 51 (1995), 5–17, 71–80.

Louit, Robert, 'Le Roman noir américain', *Magazine littéraire*, 20 (August 1968), 13–15.

Magny, Claude-Edmonde, *L'Âge du roman américain* (Paris: Seuil, 1948).

Malet, Léo (as Frank Harding), *Johnny Metal* (Paris: Ventrillard, 1941).

—— *120 rue de la gare* (Paris: SEPE, 1943).

—— (as Omer Refreger) *Derrière l'usine à gaz* (Paris: Les Éditions et revues françaises, 1944).

—— *Nestor Burma contre CQFD* (Paris: SEPE, 1945).

—— *Le Soleil n'est pas pour nous* (Paris: Éditions du Scorpion, 1949).

Manchette, Jean-Patrick, *L'Affaire N'Gustro* (Paris: Gallimard, 1971).

—— *Ô Dingos, ô châteaux!* (Paris: Gallimard, 1972).

—— *Le Petit Bleu de la côte ouest* (Paris: Gallimard, 1976).

—— *Fatale* (Paris: Gallimard, 1977).

—— 'Le Roman noir reprend des couleurs', *Nouvelles Littéraires*, (1982), 44–5.

—— 'Réponses', *Littérature*, 49 (February, 1983), 102–7.

—— 'Jean-Patrick Manchette, la position du romancier noir solitaire', *Combo* (Autumn, 1991), 7–14.

—— *Chroniques* (Paris: Éditions Payot et Rivages, 1996).

—— *La Princesse de sang* (Paris: Rivages/noir, 1996).

Mandel, Ernest, *Meurtres exquis* (Montreuil: PEC La Brèche, 1986).

Marrus, Michael, and Robert Paxton, *Vichy France and the Jews* (New York: Basic Books, 1981).

Milza, Olivier, *Les Français devant l'immigration* (Paris: Éditions Complexe, 1988).

Montalbán, Manuel Vásquez, *Southern Seas*, trans. Patrick Camiller (London: Serpent's Tail, 1986).

Morin, Edgar, *L'Esprit du temps: essai sur la culture de masse* (Paris: Grasset, 1962).

Morris, Alan, *Collaboration and Resistance Reviewed: Writers and the Mode Retro in Post-Gaullist France* (Oxford: Berg, 1992).

Mouvements, 'Dossier: Le Polar, entre critique sociale et désenchantement', 15/16 (May–August 2001).

Mullen, Anne, and Emer O'Beirne (eds.), *Crime Scenes: Detective Narratives in European Culture since 1945* (Amsterdam: Rodopi, 2000).

Munt, Sally, *Murder by the Book: Feminism and the Crime Novel* (London: Routledge, 1994).

Narcejac, Thomas, *La Fin d'un bluff: essai sur le roman policier noir américain* (Paris: Le Portulan, 1949).

Naremore, James, *More Than Night: Film Noir in Context* (Berkeley: University of California Press, 1998).

Nettelbeck, Colin, 'The "Post-Literary" Novel: Echenoz, Pennac and Company', *French Cultural Studies*, 5/2 (1994), 111–38.

Noreiko, Stephen, 'American Adaptations in the Série noire: The Case of Chandler's *The Little Sister*', *French Cultural Studies*, 8 (1997), 257–72.

—— '"Toutes des Salopes": Representation of Women in French Crime Fiction', *French Cultural Studies*, 10/1 (1999), 89–101.

Nouvelle Revue française, 'L'avenir de la fiction', 561 (April 2002).

Pennac, Daniel, *An bonheur des ogres* (Paris: Gallimard, 1985).

—— *La Fée Carabine* (Paris: Gallimard, 1987).

—— *Comme un roman* (Paris: Gallimard, 1992).

Perec, Georges, *Les Choses* (Paris: René Julliard, 1965).

Pilard, Philippe, *Henri-Georges Clouzot* (Paris: Seghers, 1969).

Piljean, André, *Passons la monnaie* (Paris: Gallimard, 1951).

Platten, David, 'Reading Glasses, Guns and Robots: A History of Science in French Crime Fiction', *French Cultural Studies*, 12/3 (October 2001), 253–70.

—— 'Polar Positions: On the Theme of Identity in Contemporary *Noir* Fiction', *Nottingham French Studies*, 41/1 (Spring 2002), 5–18.

Poe, Edgar Allan, *Selected Tales* (London: Penguin, 1994).

Polar hors séries spécial Manchette (Paris: Éditions Payots et Rivages, 1999).

Poole, Sara, '*Rompols* not of the Bailey: Fred Vargas and the *polar* as *mini-proto-mythe*', *French Cultural Studies*, 12/1 (2001), 95–108.

Porter, Charles, Foreword to 'After the Age of Suspicion: The French Novel Today', *Yale French Studies*, (1988), 1–4.

Pouy, Jean-Bernard, *La Belle de Fontenay* (Paris: Gallimard, 1992).

—— *La Petite Ecuyère à café* (Paris: La Baleine, 1995).

Prévost, Claude, and Jean-Claude Lebrun, *Nouveaux territoires romanesques* (Paris: Messidor, 1990).

Ridon, Jean-Xavier, 'Mémoire, récit et contamination dans *La Fée Carabine* de Daniel Pennac', *L'Esprit créateur*, 37/3 (Autumn 1997), 50–60.

Ross, Kristin, 'Watching the Detectives' in Frances Barker, Peter Hulme, and Margaret Inerson (eds.), *Postmodernism and the Re-reading of Modernity* (Manchester: Manchester University Press, 1992), 46–56.

—— *Fast Cars, Clean Bodies: Decolonization and the Reordering of French Culture* (Cambridge, Mass.: MIT, 1995).

Rousso, Henry, *Le Syndrome de Vichy: de 1944 à nos jours* (Paris: Seuil, 1990).

Schweighaeuser, Jean-Pierre, *Le Roman noir français* (Paris: PUF, 1984).

Silver, Alain, and James Ursini (eds.), *Film Noir: Reader 2* (New York: First Limelight Edition, 1999).

Silver, Alain, and Elizabeth Ward, *Film Noir: An Encyclopedic Reference to the American Style* (London: Secker & Warburg, 1979).

Simonin, Albert, *Touchez pas au grisbi* (Paris: Gallimard, 1953).

Siniac, Pierre, *Les Morfalous* (Paris: Gallimard, 1968).

Stewart, Terry, *La Mort et l'ange* (Paris: Gallimard, 1948).

—— *La Belle vie* (Paris: Gallimard, 1950).

Tabachnik, Maud, *Un été pourri* (Paris: Éditions Viviane Hamy, 1994).

—— 'Remarques sur la non-place des femmes dans le roman noir', *Les Temps modernes*, 595 (1997), 122–9.

Telotte, J.-P., *Voices in the Dark: The Narrative Patterns of Film Noir* (Illinois: University of Illinois Press, 1989).

Temps modernes, 'Pas d'orchidées pour les TM', 595 (August–October 1997).

Todorov, Tzvetan, 'A Typology of Detective Fiction', in *The Poetics of Prose*, trans. Richard Howard (Oxford: Blackwell, 1977), 42–52.

Tonc, Sandra, 'Questing Women: The Feminist Mystery After Feminism', in Glenwood Irons (ed.), *Feminism in Women's Detective Fiction* (London: University of Toronto Press, 1995), 46–63.

Vaillant, Luc le, 'Le Rouge-noir', *Libération*, 14 March 1997.

Vautrin, Jean, *Au bulletin rouges* (Paris: Gallimard, 1973).

Verdaguer, Pierre, *La Séduction policière: signes de croissance d'un genre réputé mineur: Pierre Magnan, Daniel Pennac et quelques autres* (Birmingham, Ala.: Summa Publications, 1999).

Vernet, Marc, 'Film Noir on the Edge of Doom', in Joan Copjec (ed.), *Shades of Noir* (London: Verso, 1999), 1–31.

Véry, Pierre, *Le Testament de Basil Crookes* (Paris: Librairie des Champs-Elysées, 1930).

Vian, Boris, *J'irai cracher sur vos tombes* (Paris: Éditions du Scorpion, 1946).

Voisard, Jacques, and Christiane Ducastelle, *La Question immigrée* (Paris: Calmann-Lévy, 1990).

Walton, Priscilla L., and Manina Jones, *Detective Agency: Women Writing the Hard-Boiled Tradition* (Berkeley: University of California Press, 1999).

—— 'Does She Or Doesn't She?: The Problematics of Feminist Detection', in Maurizio Ascari (ed.), *Two Centuries of Detective Fiction: A New Comparative Approach* (Bologna: University of Bologna, 2000), 233–59.

Waltz, Robin, 'Les Mystères de Léo Malet sous l'occupation', *Tapis-Franc: Revue du roman populaire*, 8 (1997), 116–27.

Wieviorka, Annette, *L'Ère du témoin* (Paris: Plon, 1998).

Index